AF478123

# Contemporary Fiction and the Ethics of Modern Culture

# Contemporary Fiction and the Ethics of Modern Culture

Jeffrey Karnicky

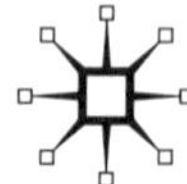

CONTEMPORARY FICTION AND THE ETHICS OF MODERN CULTURE
©Jeffrey Karnicky 2007



First published in 2007 by
PALGRAVE MACMILLAN™
175 Fifth Avenue, New York, N.Y. 10010 and
Houndmills, Basingstoke, Hampshire, England RG21 6XS.
Companies and representatives throughout the world.

PALGRAVE MACMILLAN is the global academic imprint of the Palgrave Macmillan division of St. Martin's Press, LLC and of Palgrave Macmillan Ltd. Macmillan® is a registered trademark in the United States, United Kingdom and other  countries. Palgrave is a registered trademark in the European Union and other countries.

ISBN-13: 978-1-4039-7760-1
ISBN-10: 1-4039-7760-7

Library of Congress Cataloging-in-Publication Data is available from the Library of Congress.

A catalogue record for this book is available from the British Library.

Design by Macmillan India Ltd.

First edition: March 2007

10 9 8 7 6 5 4 3 2 1

Printed in the United States of America.

*For Megan*

# CONTENTS

# ACKNOWLEDGMENTS

I appreciate the conversations with and insights provided by those who were at Penn State with me, including Marco Abel, Megan Brown, Tony Ceraso, Trey Conner, Tim Donovan, Jeremiah Dyehouse, Christine Harold, Debbie Hawhee, Jennifer Jackson, Liz Jenkins, Elizabeth Mazzolini, John Muckelbauer, Ryan Netzley, Bill Pencak, Jim Roberts, Dan Smith, Jillian Smith, Susan Squier, and Julie Vedder.

Kit Hume deserves special thanks for expert guidance in professional matters, and for helping to make this book much clearer than it would otherwise be.

Jeff Nealon also deserves special thanks for being the best theory professor ever.

I cannot thank Rich Doyle enough. This book would not exist without his insight and friendship, not to mention our many breakfasts at the Corner Room.

I also thank John McClure and Terrence Holt, who prompted me to go to graduate school.

I thank my mother, Veronica, and my father, Tony. I thank the Brown family.

I thank my editor and Palgrave and the anonymous reviewer of my manuscript.

Lastly, I thank my wife, Megan, to whom I dedicate this book.

# INTRODUCTION: ASSEMBLING AN ETHICS OF READING

I want to start with two related claims, neither of which may be true: (1) nobody reads literature anymore; (2) nobody conceptualizes reading anymore. My first claim exaggerates a line of argument that holds that during the 1980s the disparate practices that continue to be grouped under the rubric of the English department shifted away from literature and toward theory. I consider my second claim to be an effect of the first. That is, as focus shifted from literature to theory—and theory can be defined here as the study of the production of subjectivities—reading first became a subject of an intense theoretical debate that eventually dissipated so much that *reading* is no longer considered a useful term. Reading, as a site of theoretical investigation, now seems hopelessly retrograde at best, and politically naive at worst. For many, reading has come to serve as a synonym for a kind of close textual attention that is oblivious to the social, historical, and material conditions of literary production. In short, reading is no longer hip. Worse, mentions of such concepts as "response" and "ethics of reading" may throw up warning signs for many a reader fearful of a nostalgic return to such 1980s horrors as asymmetrical haircuts and "reader-response" criticism. Nevertheless, in what follows I argue that a reformulated concept of reading—focused on an ethics of response that is not just literary—can be a focal point for considering the role that literature plays in the production of subjectivities both inside and outside the academic world.

My path to an ethics of reading leads not, as might be expected, through the textual studies of Paul de Man and the "Yale school" of deconstruction, but through both the philosophical work of Maurice Blanchot, Gilles Deleuze, and Félix Guattari and the concerns of contemporary fiction. My use of "ethics" differs decidedly, in ways that I will describe below, from much work on ethics and reading. Likewise, the ways in which I employ the concepts of "reading" and "response" have little to do with reader-response criticism. I say this not to stake a claim for the originality of my position. Rather, I want to highlight my ignorance (until starting this project, that is) of the fairly recent concerns of literary theory. For a student beginning graduate studies in 1995, as I did, any knowledge of the theoretical debates surrounding reader-response criticism would have to come from archival work. That is, few graduate seminars in the mid- to late 1990s were concerned with any theoretical questions surrounding "reading." The thousands of pages devoted to such concerns in the 1980s, primarily in *Diacritics* and *New Literary History,* appear to have been forgotten by the mid-1990s.

What happened? Many would say that the advent of cultural studies and its attention to extraliterary artifacts marked the decline of literary theory, and for that matter, literature, within English departments. To make such a claim would provide a neat linear narrative of recent institutional history. Of course, that is precisely the problem of such a claim: it is just too neat and clean. The actual story of what happened as reading has moved from the center to the periphery of academic interest would certainly prove to be a much messier affair.

Rather than adapting the wide scope of inquiry that would be necessary to produce a dense institutional history of reading that might be capable of answering such a question, I want to narrow my focus here to a single question: How has the conceptualization of reading, over the past twenty-five years or so, affected the present day practice of English? I consider this question a genealogical one, in the sense that Foucault identifies the goal of genealogy:

> to identify the accidents, the minute deviations—or conversely, the complete reversals—the errors, the false appraisals, and the faulty calculations that give birth to those things that continue to exist and have value for us; it is to discover that truth or being do not lie at the root of what we know and what we are, but the exteriority of accidents. (Foucault 146)

That is, in considering the question of reading, I am not searching for a single point in time where I can say, "Here is the moment where reading lost its centrality." Nor do I seek a totalizing narrative that would ground the present in the past. I will not argue that reading has moved in a straight line from primary concern to tangential issue as time has passed. I say, in the first sentence of this introduction, that neither of my claims "may be true" for precisely this reason. To mourn the death of reading, to say that reading has reached the end of the line, would be profoundly useless. At the same time, I *do* want to argue that a rigorous conception of reading, although of seemingly little concern these days, can become a tool for both literary and cultural theorists.

In considering the role that reading has played, I want to map the movements of two tangled lines that cut through the recent history of the concept in various ways: (1) the (false) movement of centrality from reader to text to interpretive community; (2) the place of ethics in relation to reading. Working with these two lines will certainly not provide an exhaustive historical overview of reading. At the same time, I hope that close attention to them will allow me to map some of the effects that the recent history of reading has on the present. These lines overlap, mutate, die out, and leap around in various ways, but they indisputably have an effect on what counts as theory and criticism today. Following the intersections of these dead ends and lines of escape, I hope to create a line that leads toward an ethics of reading, toward a space where ethics, reading, and life mutually infect one another.

## First Line: Text–Reader–Interpretive Community

The title of Jane Tompkins's 1980 edited collection, *Reader-Response Criticism: From Formalism to Post-Structuralism,* neatly summarizes her main argument that, as literary theory moved from New Criticism to reader-response criticism, critical attention shifted from the text to the reader and finally to the "interpretive community." Tompkins notes in her introduction that "the later reader-response critics" (xxv) moved away from purely textual concerns by "relocating meaning first in the reader's self and then in the interpretive strategies that constitute it" (xxv). In this narrative, reader-response criticism finds its roots in a reversal of W. K. Wimsatt Jr. and Monroe Beardley's "The Affective Fallacy," which claims that a "confusion between the poem and its results . . . ends in impressionism and relativism" (qtd. in Tompkins ix). Reader-response criticism begins in just such a shift, from a text to the effects it produces in its readers. While various critics see different implications in this shift, one implication invariably holds true. Tompkins writes that "instead of being seen as instrumental to the understanding of the text, the reader's activity is declared to be *identical with* the text and therefore itself becomes the source of all literary value" (xvi). As the reader's experience becomes central, the kinds of questions that literary theory must ask undergo a sea change.

Reading, rather than being a search for inherent meaning, now asks, "How do readers make meaning?" (xvii). Such a question leads to another shift, away from individual readers' responses to texts, to the conventions and social systems that readers internalize. Stanley Fish's *Is There a Text in This Class? The Authority of Interpretive Communities*, published the same year as Tompkins's book, is a marker of this shift. Fish's overview of the movement from text to reader to interpretive community is strikingly similar to Tompkins's narrative, except that for Fish the narrative is a "personal history" (17) rather than an institutional one. Starting with a refutation of the affective fallacy, Fish writes, "I substituted the structure of the reader's experience for the formal structures of the text" (2). This substitution leads directly to the shift from reader to interpretive community. Fish writes that "the crucial step will be to see that the claims of neither the text nor the reader can be upheld, because neither has the independent status that would make its claims possible" (12). In other words, both texts and readers are part of a larger interpretive community that informs the creation of meaning. Fish writes that "since the thoughts an individual can think and the mental operations he can perform have their source in some or other interpretive community, he is as much a product of that community (acting as an extension of it) as the meanings it enables him to produce" (14). Of this shift, Tompkins succinctly writes, "The self as an independent entity vanishes" (xxvi). And again, this shift creates a new area of inquiry.

The social and linguistic structures that are constitutive of both texts and selves take center stage here, so that "meaning is a consequence of being in a particular situation in the world" (Tompkins xxv). This final shift, then, breaks literary theory wide open. No longer limited to purely textual considerations, reader-response criticism becomes interested in the "perception of language as a form of power" (Tompkins 226). For Tompkins, writing in 1980, such a perception "promises the most for criticism's future" (226). This perception, in a sense, *is* criticism's future in 1980. If language is considered as a form of power, every usage of language becomes a possible area of inquiry. Fish writes that criticism, considered as a form of "persuasion" (Fish 17)—that is, as a means of effecting change through language—must "account" for "everything": "texts, authors, periods, genres, canons, standards, agreements, disputes, values, changes and so on" (17). In other words, the line that moves from text to reader to interpretive community is a line of *proliferation* and *expansion*. More accounting leads to more and more meanings.

Such a line explains how "English" has moved from being a marker of close textual study to a marker of an ever-expanding field of extratextual considerations. In his 1998 *Reception Histories: Rhetoric, Pragmatism, and American Cultural Politics*, Steven Mailloux discusses the proliferating effects of reader-response criticism. He writes, "In the 1980s . . . pressured by various feminist, Marxist, New Historicist, and other sociopolitical criticisms, reader-oriented theory and practice turned more and more to the historical context and the political aspects of readers reading" (76). Here again, we have the same story of a movement from inside (the text) to outside (context). Such a movement seems to be the dominant narrative of the recent history of English. Of course, this narrative is somewhat simplified.[1] My goal here is not to complicate this narrative, or even to question its validity.

Rather than focusing on charges of oversimplification or truth or validity, I want to consider this narrative's use. Even the brief retracing that I have just done points toward the value of this narrative line: to move from the inside to the outside is to become a better reader; to account for "everything" that goes into the production of meaning seems to give a fuller, more accurate account of the ways that power works through language. In other words, it is just plain useful to pay attention to context. Tompkins notes that "reader-response critics have extended the power and usefulness of the interpretive model that they inherited from formalism" (211). Mailloux expands on just what this use might be when he discusses the now common understanding of

> how reading is historically contingent, politically situated, institutionally imbedded, and materially conditioned; of how reading

any text, literary or non-literary, relates to a larger cultural politics that goes well beyond some hypothetical private interaction between an autonomous reader and an independent text; and of how our particular views of reading relate to the liberatory potential of literacy and the transformative power of education. (78)

In this model, reading, as it expands its range from text to context, moves toward liberation and an understanding of the workings of power. What remains unquestioned here is the seemingly commonsensical progress inherent in the movement from the textual to the extratextual. It is precisely at this point that the second line I want to pursue—the dead-end line of a de Manian ethics of reading—intersects with and perhaps cuts off the proliferation of the text–reader–interpretive community line.

## Second Line: Ethics of Reading

If the first line I discuss is one of *proliferation* and *expansion* leading toward understanding, the second is one of *involution* and *stoppage* leading toward a breakdown. Right at the beginning of his 1979 book *Allegories of Reading: Figural Language in Rousseau, Nietzsche, Rilke and Proust*, de Man gets at the problem of the kinds of historical narratives I consider above. The first lines of his preface state that

> *Allegories of Reading* started out as a historical study and ended up as a theory of reading. I began to read Rousseau seriously in preparation for a historical reflection on Romanticism and found myself unable to progress beyond local difficulties of interpretation. In trying to cope with this, I had to shift from historical definition to the problematics of reading. (ix)

Why does de Man start by detailing this shift in focus? He could just as easily have started by saying, "*Allegories of Reading* is a theory of reading." Something about this shift must be important, but de Man notes that it is "of more interest in its results than in its causes" (ix). In other words, he is not interested in historicizing his shift in thought. Nor am I. What I find to be crucial here is the interruption of one line of thought, the historical, by another, the local, as if these two lines cannot exist simultaneously, as if the local cuts off access to the historical.

For de Man, this disjunction between the historical and the local is perhaps the key question for literary studies. *Allegories of Reading* dwells within this opposition as a means of deconstructing it. That is, de Man continually argues that this disjunction—whether formulated as historical/local, as I do here, or as outside/inside, rhetoric/grammar, or meaning/form, as de Man variously does—cannot ever be fully reconciled. It is this impossibility of reconciliation that prevents de Man from writing a historical study. He argues that reading can never fully and completely move from the inside of a text to the outside of its context. He writes,

> Behind the assurance that valid interpretation is possible, behind the recent interest in writing and reading as potentially effective speech acts, stands a highly respectable moral imperative that strives to reconcile the internal, formal, private structures of literary language with their external, referential, and public effects. (3)

For de Man this "striv[ing] to reconcile" always remains impossible precisely because "assurance that valid interpretation is possible" relies too heavily on a model that moves all too quickly toward a reconciliation of irreconcilable terms. Thus, for de Man, the ethical becomes an interruption of the drive toward understanding. In terms of the first line I discuss above, the line of ethics disrupts the movement from text to interpretive community, from inside to outside, by asserting that such a movement remains beholden to an unquestioned formalist system. De Man writes that "the recurrent debate opposing intrinsic to extrinsic criticism stands under the aegis of an inside/outside metaphor that is never being seriously questioned" (5). Not questioning this metaphor, for de Man, leads to groundless assumptions about the work that literary criticism can do. Any reading based on such groundless assumptions would be an unethical reading. An ethical reading practice, on the other hand, would "seriously question" any and all grounding metaphors. In fact, a de Manian ethical reading may never get past this kind of questioning.

In other words, de Man's deconstructive reading[2] endlessly short-circuits interpretation by claiming that reading is impossible when it seeks a complete understanding or "valid interpretation" of the movement from text to context, of the movement from a work of literature to a critical understanding of that work. He writes that "the attraction of reconciliation [of form and meaning, of text and context] . . . accounts for the metaphorical model of literature as a kind of box that separates an inside from an outside, and the reader or critic as the person who opens the lid in order to release in the open what was secreted but inaccessible inside" (5). Reading, for de Man, can never reach this reconciliation. Thus, reading becomes a series of endless reversals that lead not toward truth or understanding, but toward a space where it is "impossible to give an answer" that would ground any reading. In a sense, it is impossible to read de Man here. One would have to cite his readings at length to illustrate the constant undermining of interpretation by the very terms that interpretation employs. What is important for this discussion is where all readings lead for de Man.

He ends his reading of Proust[3] by stating that "*A la recherche du temps perdu* narrates the flight of meaning, but this does not prevent its own meaning from being, incessantly, in flight" (78). That is, the flight of meaning that de Man finds in Proust cannot be said to be the meaning of the work, because such an assertion would rest on an unjustified ground of meaning. This incessant flight leads a reader of de Man to a question: Where do we end up if we read ethically, if we continually question the metaphors that ground our readings? De Man argues that

> we end up . . . in the same state of suspended ignorance. Any question about the rhetorical mode of a literary text is always a rhetorical question which does not even know whether it is really questioning. The resulting pathos is an anxiety (or bliss, depending on one's momentary mood or individual temperament) of ignorance. (19)

We end up in ignorance or bliss, depending on our reaction to the impossibility of reading, on how we react to de Man's claim that no reading can ever ground itself in the truth. In other words, reading never reaches a point where "truth" can fully trump "ignorance." De Man's ethical line of reading continually doubles back on itself as it continually fails to reconcile the metaphors that it continually takes for granted. De Man cannot produce a historical study because "the problematics of reading" can never be rendered unproblematic. A de Manian reading "is condemned (or privileged) to be forever the most rigorous and, consequently, the most unreliable language in terms of which man names and transforms the world" (19).

In a sense, then, ethics for de Man is all about a continual acknowledgment that a reading can never be finalized in an interpretation. In the case of my brief discussion of reading, an ethical de Manian reading would have to constantly assert that the second line of ethics continually undermines any claims that the first line of movement from text to interpretive community would make. Any reading that would make a claim to understanding via a route from inside to outside would be groundless and unethical. I wish to make no such claims. I do, however want to dwell on this de Manian impasse and attempt to map some of its effects. That is, if one of the consequences of following the de Manian line of ethics is the constant interruption of the line that moves from inside to outside, I want to ask the following questions: How has this impasse affected the concept of reading? What has been produced by the movement away from text (the self-contained work) to context (the historical and political events surrounding the text) and by the very questioning of this movement as it is happening?

## The Literary Studies/Cultural Studies Divide, and Ethics

Just as the movement from self-contained text to material context often gets portrayed as liberatory, so does the purported movement from literary studies to cultural studies. Herbert Benítez Pezzolano, in his essay "Resistance to Literature," offers a succinct description of the literary studies/cultural studies divide: "To speak about literature within the field of Cultural Studies, or worse, to delineate an object of study that would be literature as an aesthetic discourse (according to which there would still be a need to propose something like literary studies) have become activities that fall under suspicion of idealism" (95). Such a critique is well documented, and few would argue with the productive power of pointing out the elitist, "exclusive and overspecialized" (Miklitsch 258) nature of the category "literature." To speak of "literature" without quotation marks naturalizes the material conditions and history of the concept and hearkens back to an age of literary criticism marked by close textual attention to literary texts that have no connection to the world. Cultural studies serves as a corrective here, as it deprivileges both literature and reading. In a *PMLA* "Forum" on "the actual or potential connections between cultural studies and literary studies" (257), Cary Nelson notes that a deprivileging of the literary might be of central importance to the role of cultural studies in English departments, "for we do not yet know what it would mean for the discipline to make cultural studies central and serve it fully, though it might mean that literature would no longer be our main preoccupation" (276). Nelson's tentativeness here ("it might mean") is not shared by other members of the "Forum." Many practitioners of cultural studies eagerly argue that cultural studies has already (in 1997) successfully displaced literature. As one critic notes, "As the social authority of the literary has become threatened, literary criticism has begun to appear a parsimonious discipline, with few gifts to bestow except the pleasure of reading" (Shankar 261). Lennard J. Davis writes that, as the literary loses its centrality, "literature becomes, as it should be, one practice among many, a way of witnessing human experience and conflict that is no more sacred than any other" (259); another "Forum" participant notes that "as practiced in departments of literature, cultural studies is a radical revision of literary criticism, reducing literary phenomena to symptoms of a larger cultural terrain" (Shankar 260).

Such would seem to be the end of the story. Cultural studies wins out and literary studies is left to an old guard of critics who will celebrate the "pleasures of the text." The story, of course, does not end here. John Brenkman, in his essay "Extreme Criticism," argues that viewing the literary and the cultural as oppositional fields ultimately proves fruitless:

> As soon as cultural studies is pitted against "the literary," literary studies is reduced to either its most formalistic or its most ineffable dimension. Worse yet, it is cast out of any meaningful relation to politics. Except negatively: the proponents of cultural studies castigate the elitism of literature, while the defenders of literature fend off the intrusions of politics and ideology. (116)

The debate continues on and on, with no resolution in sight. At the same time, focusing on the de Manian ethical impasse that would question the possibility of a complete move from the inside of literary studies to the outside of cultural studies can help to alter the terms of the debate.

In "The Function of Literary Theory at the Present Time,"
J. Hillis Miller delineates the line of movement from literary
studies to cultural studies as a movement from the "intrinsic" to
the "extrinsic." "In fact there has been a massive shift of the
focus in literary study since 1979 away from the 'intrinsic'
rhetorical study of literature toward study of the 'extrinsic' relations of literature, its placement within psychological, historical
or sociological contexts" (385). While noting this movement,
Miller wants at the same time to problematize it. Rather than
focusing strictly on the liberatory potential of the "extrinsic," he
locates a difficulty centered on what he calls "the actual hard
work of reading":

> All honor to the motivations which underlie this shift, this noble
> desire for social justice, for the improvement of the situation of
> women and minorities, for a clear understanding of the ideologi-
> cal presuppositions which invariably manipulate us, of which the
> shift in commitment I am describing is surely a conspicuous
> example. And all honor to the impatience with *the actual hard
> work of reading,* this nagging sense that reading may be cut off
> from the real obligations of life, the desire to make the study of
> literature somehow count, have effects of power in society and
> history. (385, emphasis added)

Miller's "actual hard work of reading" can serve as an interruption of what seems to be an unresolvable "debate" between literary and cultural studies. This focus on reading shifts discussion
from a question of what should be studied (either literary or cultural texts) to a question of what an engagement with any sort
of text can produce. In other words, an interrogation of reading
as a concept might prove useful to both literary and cultural
studies, especially if the ethical component of reading becomes
central. Rather than endless debate over what should be read, a
focus on reading asks what I would call a more important question: How does the practice of reading create actual effects in
the world? As I will discuss below, I consider this question to be
the beginning of an ethical reading.

For Miller, reading is "hard," in a sense, precisely because
reading has an ethical component. He formulates reading as two
sorts of problems—both related to ethics—that continually
threaten to cancel each other out. That is, reading can be read as
a problem of language and as a problem of action. The language

problem, which is thoroughly de Manian, dwells on the impossibility of working outside language. Any act of reading is doomed to ultimate failure because one can never reach a vantage point outside language. Miller maps out this line of argument:

> It is impossible to get outside the limits of language by means of language. Everything we reach that seems outside language, for example, sensation and perception, turns out to be more language. To live is to read, or rather to commit again and again the failure to read which is the human lot. We are hard at work trying to fulfill the impossible task of reading from the moment we are born until the moment we die. (59)

Miller's intent here is not to say that de Man always remains trapped in this language impasse. Elsewhere, he argues that such a claim is patently wrong.[4] Likewise, I do not wish to dwell on the "impossibility" of reading. Rather, what I find most interesting here is how Miller, following de Man, moves from the "intrinsic" problem of language to the "extrinsic" problem of life. That is, what I find most intriguing about the above quotation is the phrase "to live is to read." This connection between reading and living seems to be a problem of action, and thus, a problem of ethics.

In *The Ethics of Reading,* Miller writes that "the ethical moment in reading leads to an act. It enters into the social, institutional, political realms, for example in what the teacher says to the class or in what the critic writes" (4). This focus on "acts" shows how reading produces effects in the world. A critic writing or a teacher speaking before a class can directly influence the ways that a text gets read. Such acts can even affect how a student or a reader understands the concept of reading. Broadening the scope here, moving away from the more or less direct acts of teachers and critics, makes the mapping of acts more difficult. To generalize from Miller's specific examples, one could say that "acts of reading affect others." Such a claim leads to another question: What kind of a relationship to otherness does reading produce?

This question is not easily answered, even as the connection between literature and life, between an act of reading and otherness, seems to be at the center of any ethical reading. In his *Narrative Ethics,* Adam Zachary Newton considers just how this connection might function. He argues that fiction "inhabits" an ethical world, as it "manifest[s] certain characteristics which resemble features of everyday communicative experience" (25). In other words, for Newton, reading fiction is one form of inter-subjectivity among others. Fiction points to the possibility of a kind of self-creation: "Literary fiction, then, simply echoes a self-fictionalization already intact as a possibility for ordinary human interaction" (55). While Newton's work makes a convincing case that ethics is an important component of reading fiction, I argue that he undertheorizes the connections between literature and life. "Like it or not," he writes, "some version of 'reflection' has to describe the mediation of text by life and life by text" (54). In this configuration, fiction becomes a means for imagining other-ness through communicative experience. It provides access to an imagined world through which readers can explore "the extent and limits of intersubjective knowledge in persons' reading of each other" (25). I am not convinced, though, that reading engenders such a straightforward kind of intersubjectivity.

I want to argue that reading must continually question how connections to otherness get forged through the act of reading. I want to locate the ethical moment in reading at precisely this spot, in the solitary encounter that produces a movement from reading to action, from text to world, from literature to life. Simply put, I want to argue that reading's relation to otherness resides somewhere between the "suspended ignorance" of a de Manian ethics and the "everyday communicative experience" of critics such as Newton. The works of Gilles Deleuze, Félix Guattari, and Maurice Blanchot can point to other ways of for-mulating the solitary encounter between literature and life that happens with every act of reading.

## Reading and Otherness

As I have discussed above, de Man continually deconstructs "the metaphorical model of literature as a kind of box that separates an inside from an outside" (5) without offering any way out of this binary. Reading always "fails" because it can never reconcile the very binary oppositions that are at the center of every act of reading. In "Letter to a Harsh Critic," Deleuze writes of two ways of reading. The first, which he wants to reject, works when one sees a book "as a box with something inside and start[s] looking for what it signifies, and then if you're even more perverse or depraved you set off after signifiers" (8). He argues that this way of reading remains bound up in the textual, so that "you treat the next book like a box contained in the first or containing it. And you annotate and interpret and question and write a book about the book, and so on and on" (7–8). Such a way of reading can never move from inside to outside. Within this metaphoric understanding of literature as a box, all acts of reading, no matter how much they might attempt to flee the textual, remain bound up in language.

Rather than attempting to reconcile the binary oppositions inherent in the "literature as box" metaphor, Deleuze offers another way of thinking about reading. In this formulation, reading becomes "like plugging into an electric circuit":

> There's the other way: you see the book as a little non-signifying machine, and the only question is 'does it work, and how does it work?' How does it work for you? . . . This second way of reading's intensive: something comes through or it doesn't. There's nothing to explain, nothing to understand, nothing to interpret. It's like plugging into an electric circuit . . . This second way of reading's quite different from the first, because it relates a book directly to what's Outside. A book is a little cog in much more complicated external machinery. Writing is one flow among others, with no special place in relation to the others, that comes into relations of current, countercurrent, and eddy with other flows. (8)

Deleuze's "second way of reading" argues that an engagement with literature need not proceed through a series of irreconcilable oppositions, be they inside/outside, text/reader, or literature/life. Rather, acts of reading continually reformulate such connections through asking "How does it work?" Reading neither moves in a straight line from text to world nor remains bound up in textuality. The connections formed, through reading, between a book and the world are much more difficult to map. In a sense, Deleuze's notion that a book is only one part of a "more complicated external machinery" resonates with Miller's focus on "the actual hard work of reading." Both focus on the difficulties of saying exactly how literature relates to life. More importantly, though, both refuse to simplify these connections.

To consider reading as "a little cog" in a larger apparatus by no means diminishes reading. Likewise, saying that writing is "one flow among others" does not diminish the power of writing. Instead, such a formulation removes reading and writing from the intrinsic, insular, "exclusive and overspecialized" spaces that practitioners of cultural studies critique. Deleuze's formulation claims that reading does not work as a simple solitary encounter between a reader and a text. Newton argues that the ethical moment of reading is in this solitary encounter. He writes that

> solitary reading . . . leaves all differences intact between the reader and possible but invisible others . . . Indeed, perhaps the profoundest ethical dilemma which reading fiction poses *is just* the fact of solitude, that it is accomplished alone, forcing one's own single self against and into the world(s) of fictional others. (23)

Following Deleuze's model of reading here, one can argue that it is impossible to "leave all differences intact" in an act of reading. That is, while one usually does read alone, in a kind of solitude, the lines between a reader and a possible "fictional other" are not so clear-cut. In a move that seems paradoxical, Deleuze, following Blanchot, writes that this "absolute solitude . . . is an extremely populous solitude. Populated . . . with encounters . . . It is from the depth of this solitude that you can make any encounter whatsoever. You encounter people . . . but also movements, ideas, events, entities" (Deleuze and Parnet 6). In other words, the solitary space of reading and writing is not a space where a reading self forms a one-to-one connection with a fictionalized self. The relationship to otherness created through reading is not given. The connections forged to otherness through reading are complex and varying, and difficult to comprehend or map out. Reading, as the act of making these connections, can be considered as both a creative and an ethical practice.

## Creativity and Ethics

Perhaps the strongest link among Blanchot's, Deleuze's, and Guattari's respective discussions of reading is their claim that an engagement with a text, a reading, produces real, material effects in the world. Such a claim, I argue, leads directly toward an ethics of reading. While they all use different formulations— Blanchot writes of the "objects" formed through literary encounters, Deleuze writes of "life," and Guattari writes of the "reinvention of the subject"—all three theorize reading as a complex, and productive, encounter with otherness.

In "Kafka and Literature," Blanchot writes that literature constructs "objects" that are much more than reflections or representations of the world. Using the example of "pain," Blanchot writes that literature

> objectifies pain by forming it into an object. It does not express it, it makes it exist on another level, it gives it a materiality which is no longer that of the body but the materiality of words which represent the upheaval of the world that suffering claims to be. Such an object is not necessarily an imitation of the changes that pain makes us live through: it shapes itself to *present* pain, not *represent* it; first of all, this object must exist, that is, it must be an always indeterminate conjunction of determined relationships. (20–21)

Blanchot's focus on "the materiality of words" is key here, as is his distinction between *representation* and *presentation*. If words lacked "materiality," their function would be nothing more than reflection or representation. That is, if language is considered as purely textual, one can only formulate reading as a continual failure. Reading becomes "impossible," precisely because it cannot transcend language. As a de Manian reading might say, every reading takes place *within* language and is thus ultimately *about* language. Blanchot's "object," though, is capable of producing extralinguistic effects. By "objectifying" pain (in this case), literature creates something new, an "object" that exists in the world. Blanchot characterizes this existence as "an always indeterminate conjunction of determined relationships." A literary object exists in that it reconfigures the world in some yet-to-be-known way. One cannot know beforehand what connections will be forged by a reading. Blanchot writes that

> the goal of art *is* an object—a real, that is, an effective one. Not a momentary dream, a pure inner smile, but a realized action which is itself activating, which informs or deforms others, appeals to them, affects them, moves them—towards other actions which, most often, do not return to art but belong to the course of the world. (212)

For Blanchot, the whole point of art is that it is affective. An engagement with art is always an encounter with otherness. And this encounter is always a kind of action. Whether the encounter "informs," "deforms," "appeals," "affects," or "moves," it always makes something happen. What exactly this "something" is can only be determined through the encounter, through an actual act of reading. Reading becomes a creative endeavor when it forms unforeseen connections, or creates Deleuzian lines of flight, between a work and the world. Deleuze writes that "the great and only error lies in thinking that a line of flight consists in fleeing from life; the flight into the imaginary, or into art. On the contrary, to flee is to produce the real, to create life, to find a weapon" (Deleuze and Parnet 49). Reading, in this configuration, is not an insular movement into a text. Rather, it moves toward the creation of a "life," toward something that exists and acts in the world.

Guattari, in *Chaosmosis*, configures the engagement with a work of art in a similar manner. For him, reading (or listening to music or watching television) is an "activity" that can "lead to a recreation and a reinvention of the subject itself" (131). Engaging with a work, for Guattari, is not an intellectual exercise in which one briefly imagines being other; rather, reading actively creates new ways of living in the world. It is precisely in these acts of "creation," "recreation," and "reinvention" that reading becomes ethical.

All of the acts mentioned in the above paragraph are in the realm of an ethics of reading, because they are all kinds of responses to otherness. For Deleuze, ethics starts with a questioning of our "ways of existing." He writes that "ethics is a set of optional rules that assess what we do, what we say, in relation to the ways of existing involved. We say this, do that: what way of existing does it involve" ("Life" 100). Deleuze never explicitly links ethics and reading, but such a connection is easy to forge. A Deleuzian ethics can be considered a kind of continual questioning: "What is our ethics, how do we produce an artistic experience, what are our processes of subjectification, irreducible to our moral codes? Where and how are new subjectivities being produced? What can we look for in our present day communities?" ("Portrait" 115). Asking these kinds of questions about the act of reading, I want to argue, leads directly toward an ethics of reading. In particular, in what follows, I want to focus on Deleuze's last question regarding "our present day communities." I want to ask what kinds of subjectivities are being formed both by postmodern literature and by the attempts of postmodern literary criticism.

## Against Interpretation and Clarification

Deleuze and Guattari never wrote about contemporary American or British fiction, and neither has Blanchot. Likewise, most works of postmodern literary criticism rarely cite Deleuze, Guattari, or Blanchot.[5] One critic who does write about Deleuze, Timothy Murphy, in his book-length study of William S. Burroughs, *Wising Up the Marks,* argues that Deleuze has "produced a critical language that evades the endless squabbling over terminology that marks most discussions of (post)modernism" (2). Murphy employs a Deleuze-Guattarian style of reading in an attempt to think the work of criticism differently. Rather than seek a definition of what "postmodernism" might be, Murphy "attempts to articulate an alternative to the dialectic of modernism and postmodernism . . . that dominates many discussions of American literature in the contemporary period" (1). For Murphy, Deleuze's acritical study of literature helps to provide a means for discussing postmodern literature while at the same time avoiding the "endless squabbling" of the postmodernism debate. Of course, this "endless squabbling" is, in a sense, the purpose—the institutional goal—of postmodern literary criticism: to continually replicate itself. For these reasons, Murphy notes that Deleuze's evasion of this squabbling "accounts in part for Deleuze's own relative 'invisibility' in Anglophone critical circles" (2). Likewise, Gregg Lambert notes that Deleuze's writings on literature "seem to pay no attention or even tribute to the field of criticism" (136), and thus it is hard to "imagine a 'Deleuzian school of literary theory,' understood as one approach among others in a pluralism of critical styles and methodologies, preserving the relative stability of the field of literary objects" (136).

Neither Deleuze, Guattari, nor Blanchot lend themselves to a methodological understanding of their works. In part, this is because of the acritical nature of these works. None of them is interested in producing judgments or in "understanding" literary works. For Blanchot, criticism never gets near the "essence," or the profound uselessness, of literature. Criticism, the use of literature that "expresses or . . . refutes what is generally said," (*Space*

206) in the very act of making literature a space for social reflection, effaces literature and causes it to disappear. Rather than emphasizing a critical approach toward literature, Blanchot calls for a reading that has concerns in addition to meaning and interpretation. "Reading, in the literary sense, is not even a pure movement of comprehension. It is not the interpretation that keeps meaning alive by pursuing it" (196). Reading instead "becomes the approach to the work and an utterly joyful welcome to the work's generosity" (196). This "joyful welcome" cannot be made into a methodology, according to Blanchot, since "it breaks off as soon as it ceases to be the approach toward what rules out any understanding" (198). Any reading that invokes Blanchot must attempt to engage literature as a site of constant genesis to be encountered and not as a static space of conversation to be understood and interpreted. Such a reading must take into account the ways in which the discipline of literary criticism, and particularly postmodern literary criticism, has naturalized understanding and meaning as the reasons for reading.

The final paragraph of Fredric Jameson's *Postmodernism, or the Cultural Logic of Late Capitalism* exemplifies postmodern literary criticism's drive to systematize and define, a drive that I want to strive to resist:

> The rhetorical strategy of the preceding pages has involved an experiment, namely, the attempt to see whether by systematizing something that is resolutely unsystematic, and historicizing something that is resolutely ahistorical, one couldn't outflank it and force a historical way at least of thinking about that. "We have to name the system": this high point of the sixties finds an unexpected revival in the postmodernism debate. (418)

Jameson's argument here engenders nearly all postmodern literary criticism written since 1984. Such postmodern literary criticism has become a "postmodernism debate" that strives to characterize—whether it be through economic, cultural, aesthetic, or stylistic analyses—"the system" that has produced and is simultaneously produced by postmodern literature. Consensus can easily be reached; we name the system in question—late capitalism, postmodernism—but we must now endlessly debate the signification of these names. As criticism gets caught up in this postmodernism debate, it leaves little room for a discussion of reading.

The origins of this debate cannot wholly be traced to Jameson; at the same time, Jameson's discussions of postmodernism have been, and continue to be, entry points into the discussion for most postmodern literary critics.[6] Brian McHale, whose *Postmodernist Fiction* can be considered a canonical work of postmodern literary criticism, characterizes the centrality of postmodernism. "Jameson, it seems, is always there ahead of one, his own claim clearly staked, no matter what topic in postmodern culture one has set out to investigate, so that one seems always compelled to deal with Jameson first before beginning to deal with the matter at hand" (*Constructing* 269n11). McHale's claim that Jameson must be "dealt with" is borne out from even a cursory survey of recent postmodern literary criticism.[7]

Most often, critics "deal with" Jameson by arguing that his postmodernism is static and monolithic. In *Theories of Play in Postmodern Fiction,* Brian Edwards critiques "the totalities in which [Jameson] deals that devalue the exuberance and invention in postmodernist production . . . His is a gloomy postmodernism" (83). Such "gloominess," for many critics, serves to limit the debate's terms, to shut down any positive work that the postmodern literary critic might do. As James Annesley writes, "The point is that late capitalism is a formation in which, despite its integrated appearance, contradictions and tensions still remain. The intensification of commercial activity does not inevitably lead to the production of a frozen, standardized world" (73).[8] The critic's job here becomes obvious: provide a fluid, nonstatic way of looking at postmodernism that takes into account the "contradictions and tensions" of the late capitalist world. As McHale might be quick to point out here, Jameson has this position already "staked out." Jameson argues that *every* discussion of postmodernism must begin by considering the inevitable tensions and inconsistencies engendered by the use of the word "postmodernism." He writes that "we are under the obligation to rehearse those inner contradictions and to stage those representational inconsistencies and dilemmas; we have to work that through *every time around*" (xxii, emphasis added). "Postmodernism" must, by its very nature, always be open to debate.

Such endless rehearsal easily leads toward what Richard Walsh calls "the generality of an ultraformalism" (27). That is, a discussion that constantly grounds itself in "postmodernism" inevitably diminishes the singularity of texts that come to be considered postmodern. Every postmodern text becomes an example of the fluidity of the concept. One could easily drown in the proliferation of fluid definitions of "postmodernism," or better yet, "postmodernism*s*."[9] At the same time, little gets said about the work such fluidity does. Where is this added "*s*" leading postmodern literary criticism? What's the purpose of opening the debate to a wider and wider field? For Jameson, and more importantly, for the "postmodernism debate" that finds its roots in Jameson, consensus looms on an ever-receding horizon. While warning against "premature clarification," he argues that "*Postmodernism* is not something we can settle once and for all" (xxii), at least not until "the end, and not at the beginning of our discussions of it" (xxii). This "end" rarely gets directly addressed, yet it's always there, off in the distance of some future moment where everything will be decided once and for all. In the meantime, the conversation must continue, unabated.

As the conversation continues, postmodern literary criticism often notes the fragmentary, open-ended nature of both postmodern literature and the late capitalist world that this literature represents. Yet this open-endedness serves the ultimate end of rendering postmodern literature as an object of study and brings a "relative stability" to the field. That is, even as postmodern literature is viewed as fragmentary and open ended, it is also seen as a reflection of a totalizable, knowable world. Joseph Tabbi characterizes this viewpoint. "And if the postmodern reality should turn out to be incomplete and undecidable, the loss of certainty can also produce 'a modest gain in realism about one's powers'" (*Postmodern*, 29). Open-endedness, fragmentation, incompleteness, and undecidability undermine any sort of "master narrative" that would order the postmodern world; at the same time, "postmodern reality" becomes an object of knowledge constituted by its incompleteness. An accretion of incomplete, fragmentary criticism then builds toward an inevitable, if still unreachable, consensus. McHale, in a review of Jameson's *Postmodernism*, writes that "the masterfulness of master narratives—and the consequent anxiety—can be 'turned down' in this generation by the combined efforts of all of us together" ("Postmodernism" 32). "All of us together" can produce endlessly proliferating namings of the system that produces postmodern literature, as "we" strive toward a definition—or better, definitions—of postmodern literature. The "postmodern turn" of literary criticism enables a proliferation of discourse (no master narratives) that nonetheless strives toward a totalized theory of postmodernism (as incomplete and undecidable).

Such a movement toward both proliferation and control works through what Jeffrey Nealon calls "the surreptitious forwarding of a certain institutional interest in determination *itself,* an interest in arresting what purports to be an open-ended process in the service of 'professional,' institutional ends" (3). That is, the desire "to name the system" coexists with stated efforts to resist totalizing narratives, even as this resistance serves to create an unspoken closure in the discipline. What remains unspoken is what Nealon calls "the *ends* of inquiry, the unquestioned 'useful work' that a discipline or method allows one to perform" (113). The proliferation of what McHale calls "little narratives" that "turn down" master narratives allows the discipline of postmodern literary criticism to proliferate through the production of what he calls "a strategically useful and satisfying fiction" (qtd. in Nealon 113). More and more names for the system can be argued as more and more postmodern literary criticism proliferates, just as long as such criticism is "useful and satisfying"—that is, so long as the criticism furthers the body of knowledge known as postmodern literary criticism. Postmodern literary critics must resign themselves to waiting for results as we strive to understand, order, categorize, define, and systematize a resolutely open-ended, fragmentary, and unsystematic postmodern literature. The terms of the debate become the limits of the discourse; the best one can hope to do is produce incomplete, undecidable, and useful narratives about postmodern literature while working toward some debate-ending clarification that always exists somewhere off in the future. What I hope to show in the readings that follow is that encountering postmodern literature is not a program geared toward debate and understanding, but is instead a process, a means of producing a different kind of future. The movement toward this future is not a straight line of clarification. Rather, it is a continually fluctuating line of creation.

## Programs of Life

At this point, a reader may be wondering where all of this is going. If reading does not lead toward clarification and understanding, where does it lead? What exactly do acts of reading create? Deleuze writes that "to write is certainly not to impose a form (of expression) on the matter of lived experience. Literature rather moves in the direction of the ill-formed or the incomplete" ("Literature" 1). Writing, in this configuration, works not as a representation of the world, but as a kind of creation. I argue that all of the writers I consider in this book move in this direction, away from reflections or critiques of contemporary reality and toward new configurations of subjectivity, new ways of life that are "ill-formed" and "incomplete" precisely because they are in a state of continual emergence. That is, while writers such as Susan Daitch or David Markson might create fragmentary narratives full of miscommunication and disconnection, I claim that they are not simply reflecting a fragmentary contemporary world full of miscommunication and disconnection. Likewise, while Richard Powers's characters often fail to complete goals or to have meaningful human interactions, I do not view these "failures" as reflections of the human condition in the twenty-first century. David Foster Wallace's and Irvine Welsh's characters never "self-actualize" or "come to terms" with inner conflicts, and Wallace's *Infinite Jest*, after a thousand pages, doubles back on itself instead of reaching a resolution. I do not consider these works as fragments of a missing unity. The breakdowns and impasses that populate these works of fiction are "ill-formed" and "incomplete," in that they are neither expressions of a complex reality nor symptoms of a disjointed society.

Reading these writers does not lead toward a "useful and satisfying" account of the world. Rather than attempt to reconcile the works of these writers with contemporary reality, I want to consider how they may in fact lead to an alteration of reality. Since this book is, in a sense, a work of literary criticism, an attempt to reconfigure the work of postmodern literary criticism can be seen as a kind of starting point. Rather than trying to connect these writers to a larger field of postmodern literature, I want to dwell on the impasses that each writer creates. I want to focus on how each writer, in his or her singular way, articulates new formations of subjectivity. Each chapter of this book can be read as a mapping of the conditions of emergence for these subjectivities. Such a mapping can also be read as an ethics of engagement, as a means of encountering the emergent subjectivities of postmodern fiction. Such a way of reading does not strive toward a totality that will eventually say what postmodern literature "is." Instead, my readings attempt to destabilize "the field of literary objects" and provide a strong means for engaging the singularity of postmodern literature.

I consider each work under consideration to be what Deleuze calls a "program of life." More precisely, I consider the acts of reading that I attempt to articulate in the following pages to be programs of life. Deleuze writes of a way of encountering literature in which there are

> only programs of life, always modified in the process of coming into being, betrayed in the process of being hollowed out, like banks which are disposed or canals which are arranged in order that a flux may flow . . . Programs are not manifestos—still less are they phantasms, *but means of providing reference points for an experiment which exceeds our capacities to foresee.* (Deleuze and Parnet 48)

Such programs point toward a model of postmodern literary criticism that resists entry into a "postmodernism debate" about the meaning of contemporary literature in favor of an ethical register that considers how a reader might engage with the otherness produced by and in literary texts. Reading functions as a program of life when it continually takes flight in multiple directions.

Two directions of reading seem particularly important here: the conceptual and the stylistic. In each chapter my readings attempt to enact concepts present in the literature being read. At the same time, the style in which the works under consideration present these concepts infects my writing. Chapter 1, "Between Reading and Writing: Susan Daitch, David Markson, and 'Bartleby,'" focuses on the movement between reading and writing as conceptualized by Daitch and Markson—not as a one-way movement between reading and writing, but as a continual oscillation. This chapter is a slow rumination; it dwells in the space of reading and writing, just as Blanchot and Derrida do, just as the narrators of the stories I discuss do. These stylistics infect my reading and writing style and create a new style of engagement that then varies with each ensuing chapter. In Chapter 1, I configure both reading and writing as capacities to be affected. In this chapter, I attempt to enact this very capacity, to illustrate how literary criticism can become an affective discourse.

If Chapter 1 is infected by a space of reading and writing, Chapter 2, "Fascinated Disgust in Richard Powers," is overwhelmed by the concept of fascinated disgust. In this chapter, I focus on fascinated disgust as a continually fluctuating space of response between self and other. Such a space works within the novels, I argue, but it also works on me as I write criticism. That is, it works conceptually to reconfigure subjectivity; stylistically, the space of fascinated disgust affects the working of literary criticism. The desire to say "nothing" about Powers's novels continually haunts my readings of the novels.

In Chapter 3, "Kinds of Stasis in David Foster Wallace," I look at how various movements toward stasis in Wallace's work lead toward both new configurations of subjectivity and an "asignifying stasis" that questions the unity that much postmodern literary criticism strives to create. As I catalog the continual breakdowns in Wallace's work, the chapter itself continually breaks down and starts over.

Chapter 4, "Silence Junkies: Irvine Welsh's Novel Subjectivities," maps the various ways in which the desire for silence in Welsh's characters leads to a continual renegotiation of the roles that politics, psychology, and society play in the creation of subjects. At the same time, Welsh's characters resist any sort of analysis. My readings of these characters continually runs up against their desire for silence as I attempt to negotiate the difficulties of saying anything at all about Welsh's work.

The authors that I write about do not necessarily add up to any sort of postmodern canon. Rather, I consider each author as producing singular enunciations that must be encountered on their own terms. Each novel and short story insists on its own singularity. There is certainly not one single way to read. In my conclusion, I discuss how an ethics of reading that resists generalization can work pedagogically.

Considered as an ethical negotiation among social contexts, *reading* might function as a powerful tool. Readings can create openings for the emergence of subjectivities that reconfigure the functions of contemporary politics and culture in what Deleuze calls "unforeseen and nonpreexistent" ways. Each of the following chapters can be read as a response cultivated by the texts I have read, a response that demands a creative integration of form and content. An ethics of reading is assembled as it continually breaks down; thus, an ethics of reading must be rebuilt with each reading, with close attention paid to the singularity of each text. Each of the readings that follow is a "program of life," in that it is an assemblage, in that it is only produced as it is run, always ill-formed and incomplete, not driven toward a specific end. I want to claim that an ethics of reading cannot be described in the abstract. It cannot precede an act of reading. An ethics of reading postmodern literature cannot be generalized. It only becomes clear as it emerges through singular acts of reading.

# Between Reading and Writing: Susan Daitch, David Markson, and "Bartleby"

*What most threatens reading is this: the reader's reality, his personality, his immodesty, his stubborn insistence upon remaining himself in the face of what he reads—a man who knows in general how to read.*

—*Maurice Blanchot,* The Space of Literature, *198*

*To write is also to become something other than a writer.*

—*Gilles Deleuze, "Literature and Life," 6*

## Writing Is Read

The sentence "I woke up to find Gregor Samsa in my sink" (Daitch 9) actualizes three readers: Susan Daitch, from whose story "Killer Whales" the sentence comes (it is the first sentence of the story); the nameless narrator of the story who refers to the cockroach in her sink as Gregor Samsa; and me, as I encounter the sentence on the page.

From reading this sentence, I assume that Susan Daitch has read Franz Kafka's short story "The Metamorphosis," since Daitch's sentence is a rewriting of the translated first sentence of "The Metamorphosis." Likewise, I can assume that the narrator of "Killer Whales" has read Kafka's story, since the narration is in a first-person voice. And as I simultaneously recognize the allusion as I read the sentence, I can assume that I have read both Kafka's story and Daitch's story. I *say* that I have read "The Metamorphosis," but I cannot recall exactly when or where I read the story. All of these assumptions work indirectly; as I read the sentence, I can trace no exact route back to Kafka's story. A chain of indirect discourse links these three readers to Kafka's sentence as translated by Willa and Edwin Muir: "As Gregor Samsa awoke one morning from uneasy dreams he found himself transformed in his bed into a gigantic insect" (89).

Of course, the possibility of an infinite number of readers can be inferred from this sentence. The actual number, somewhere between three and infinity, finds its limit in such things as the number of copies of the story in print, the number of photocopies of the story made in violation of copyright and so on, with "and so on" serving as a reminder of what Derrida calls the "essential iterability" ("Signature" 20) of a written sign. Simply put, a written thing, by necessity, must be repeatable in order to be readable. There must always be more than one possible reader for something to function as writing. Another sentence of Kafka's, this time read by Maurice Blanchot, can help prove this seemingly obvious point. In reading Kafka's sentence "He was looking out the window," Blanchot notes that this is "a sentence that belongs to other people, people who can read it" (Blanchot, "Literature 305–306). Blanchot can read Kafka's sentence, I can read Blanchot's citation of Kafka, and anybody reading this can read my citation of Blanchot citing Kafka.

Reading is the affirmation of writing, the acknowledgment that writing exists. I become a reader the moment I encounter any of the sentences I cite above. At the same time, something more happens in the act of reading. Blanchot notes that a sentence "belongs to" those who read it. Writing incites a response beyond mere reader acknowledgment. To read is to be affected by writing, to do something with writing. "I woke up to find Gregor Samsa in my sink" renders distinguishable effects in everyone who reads the sentence. For instance, recognition of the allusion to "Gregor Samsa" sets up an identifiable limit, a specific context in which Daitch's story can be read. Recognition creates a capacity to be affected in specific ways by the sentence and the story that it begins. Not "getting" the allusion, or being unaware that an allusion exists, might produce confusion—What is a being with the name Gregor Samsa doing in the sink?—or even annoyance. Of course, such a misrecognition certainly still qualifies as a reading. I would like to bracket misreading for the moment[1], in the service of the conclusion that reading can be defined as *a capacity to be affected* by a written text.

Discussable effects are produced in those readers who recognize the allusion to Kafka. A knowledge of Gregor Samsa sets limits on Daitch's story, so that "Killer Whales" cannot mean anything or nothing to any reader; without these limits, without an identifiable context, a reading of the story would be impossible. But readings are possible. I recognize the allusion and I think that "Killer Whales" will probably be "Kafkaesque" in some sense. Further, because of the oblique way in which Daitch's first sentence is a rewrite of Kafka's first sentence, I note that I am about to undertake the reading of a story that could perhaps be called "postmodern." Following this train of thought, I can also note the metonymic quality of the signifier Gregor Samsa; that is, in the sentence under discussion, the name "Gregor Samsa" signifies "cockroach." Because of this equation, I anticipate a flattening of any metaphorical, or even metaphysical, exploration that might have been produced in Kafka's story. I can also note the juxtaposition of what has become a canonical short story and the sheer everydayness of a roach appearing in a sink to further shore up my sense that I am reading a postmodern story. Then I can infer that "Killer Whales" might in fact be a postmodern story about reading, since I know that the narrator of the story is a reader who playfully cites earlier texts. And I know this about the narrator before I even know his or her name.

I infer correctly. "Killer Whales" concerns itself with reading. The story interrogates what it means to read, what the purpose of reading might be, and what effects reading produces in readers. Before continuing with my reading, I want to pause and question precisely how reading the first sentence of "Killer Whales" led to the almost instantaneous inferences I make above. How does the sentence come to "belong to" me so that I write about it at length? What happens in the instant of reading to set the mind racing?

* * *

Reading certainly invites reflection. One often reads, and then pauses to consider what has just been read; one easily returns at a later date to explore readings that took place an hour ago, yesterday, or weeks or months ago. At the same time, reading entails a certain immediacy. In the moment of reading, one becomes a reader. I use "reader" here in a specific sense that is not to be confused with the notion of being a reader as a quality of an individual, as when someone who enjoys reading and reads a lot says, "I'm an avid reader." My interest here does not lie in the continual process of being a reader, but in the moment of reading when one becomes a reader. Deleuze and Guattari's concept of "incorporeal transformations," while not a concept they relate to reading, can shed light on this moment.

For Deleuze and Guattari, "the incorporeal transformation is recognizable by its instantaneousness, its immediacy, by the simultaneity of the statement expressing the transformation and the effect the transformation produces" (*Thousand* 81). For example, Deleuze and Guattari note that one who is accused of a crime becomes a convict in the "pure instantaneous act" of the judge's reading of the sentence. Calling the transformation from accused to convict instantaneous and incorporeal does not discount the committing of the crime, the trial or the carrying of the sentence, or the very real corporeal effects of the transformation. Rather, a focus on the moment of instantaneous transformation illustrates the power of a singular speech act. A judge or jury stating "guilty" renders the accused a convict as the verdict is being read. Likewise, Deleuze and Guattari write that "love is an intermingling of bodies . . . but the declaration 'I love you' expresses a noncorporeal attribute of bodies, the lover's as well as the loved ones" (81). Such a statement certainly can produce physical alterations in the bodies involved, but only after the immediate transformation that the speech act orders. Using the example of an airplane hijacking, Deleuze and Guattari note that while there are physical actions involved, the waving of guns, the killing of hostages, and "the transformation of the passengers into hostages, and of the plane-body into a prison-body, is an instantaneous incorporeal transformation, a 'mass media act'" (81).

In writing of incorporeal transformation, Deleuze and Guattari are concerned with enunciated statements, or speech acts: "Guilty," "I love you." But, these "statement[s] expressing the transformation" that a body undergoes need not be sentences enunciated by a speaker. In his novel *Underworld*, Don DeLillo diagrams two incorporeal transformations that take place during a baseball game—in this case, the New York Giants' historic, pennant-winning game of October 3, 1951. Standing at the plate, a batter is described as being in "the trance of waiting" for the pitcher to throw the ball (27). Everything is suspended; nothing is happening in this moment. But this nothingness engenders what comes next.

> The difference comes when the ball is hit. Then nothing is the same. The men are moving, coming out of their crouches, and everything submits to the pebble-skip of the ball, to rotations and backspins and airstreams . . . There are things that apply unrepeatedly, muscle memory and pumping blood and jots of dust, the narrative that lives in the . . . play-by-play . . . And the crowd is also lost in this space, the crowd made over in that one-thousandth of a second when the bat and the baseball are in contact. (27–28)

In the instant, the "one-thousandth of a second," the bat hitting the ball starts, and with subsequent pitches, restarts, the game. The men on the field become baseball players; the group of people in the stands become a crowd watching a game. In baseball "nothing is the same" every time the ball is hit. Even as this is working "unrepeatedly," it repeats. Another pitch is thrown; another bat makes contact. Waiting then playing. Waiting then playing. The incorporeal transformation occurs repeatedly and differently each time as the game progresses; the game is made of the repetition of these singular, unrepeatable moments of incorporeal transformation.

Likewise, reading and writing. There's that one-thousandth of a second when reading and writing are in contact, when eyes meet words, and also when fingers meet keys: the muscle memory of the keyboard's layout, the unthinking action of the eye scanning the page, the almost automatic movement of the hand turning the page. In these instants everything changes. Waiting, then reading. Waiting, then writing. Waiting. Writing. Waiting. Reading. Waiting. Writing.

* * *

The unthinking repetition of unrepeatable moments happens every time I read. I am rendered a reader as a sentence affects me—as my eyes contact words on a page. Following from these instants, associations are called forth. A batter swings and hits the ball; a reader reads and associations are called forth. Of course, a batter often swings and misses, but the game still happens. Likewise, a reading can produce few or no associations—who is Gregor Samsa?—but reading still happens. The difference between reading and misreading is the difference between hitting the ball and swinging and missing. And if one considers the nearly infinite possibilities of a batter's response to a thrown pitch—ground ball, line drive, pop-up, single, double, triple, home run, out, double play, foul ball, etc.—one can also see the nearly infinite possibilities of a reader's response to a written text. Within the rules of the game, some responses are judged as better than others. In most situations, a player would rather hit a home run than strike out, and a reader would rather know who Gregor Samsa is in order to form a group of associations relating to the significance of this knowledge. Of course, not "getting" an allusion need not lead to an impoverished reading, just as not hitting a home room need not be considered a failed at bat. A missed allusion by no means necessarily decreases one's capacity to be affected by a text.

It is also important to consider that the very possibility of playing the game—of a hitter stepping in to face a pitcher— results from the limits imposed by the game's rules. While the results of an at bat are nearly limitless, they are circumscribed by a very distinct set of unchanging rules. Likewise, a text cannot work in just any way. This is not to say that the rules of reading can be codified in the sense that the rules of baseball are, although certainly some people have wished this were the case. Rather, readings are made possible by limitations that are in constant variation and dependent on the context of the reading. Deleuze and Guattari note that "'I swear!' . . . is a different statement depending on whether it is said by a child to his father, by a man in love to his loved one, or by a witness before the court" (*Thousand* 94). In each case, the statement works differently to produce varying effects. These variations produced by the same statements lead Deleuze and Guattari toward a pragmatics of language that rejects the notion that "the variables are merely situational, and that the statement remains constant in principle" (94). For them, the statement is not defined by a grammatical rule. Instead, it is considered in the context of its continual variation, in the unrepeatable instant of its utterance. "To place the statement in continuous variation is to send it through all the prosodic, semantic, syntactical, and phonological variables that can affect it in the shortest moment of time" (94). Instantaneous variation produces specific effects that cannot be predetermined: the way a baseball game will play out cannot be determined beforehand by the knowledge of its rules; rather, the rules of the game are the ground for the continuous variation that takes place in each transforming moment of the game. Likewise, no "constant principle" can tell us what a statement means; we can only build what Deleuze and Guattari call an "internal pragmatics" (94) that is immanent to language. That is, the meaning of "I swear!" is bound up in the transformations that the utterance of the phrase produces. "I swear!" has different meanings because it produces differing contextual effects when said in different circumstances, as when the child swears before his father or the witness swears to tell the truth. Likewise, the meaning of reading is to be found in the varying, instantaneous transformations produced in the act of reading. Reading is a process of continual variation played out in the encounter between reader and text, just as baseball is a process of continual variation played out in the encounter between pitcher and batter. Pitches are hit. Writing is read.

Or, "writing is read" (Derrida, "Signature" 21), to give credit to Jacques Derrida for this dense statement that links reading and writing. I want to consider the connections between reading and writing that Derrida articulates with "is." Even as the sentence "I woke up to find Gregor Samsa in my sink" renders me a reader, I find myself writing as well. I move from reader to writer in the flash of a cursor. What kind of movement is this? What is the relationship between becoming a reader and becoming a writer? When does one become a writer? When the words are written? Or when they are read? Or do reading and writing happen simultaneously? Must one precede the other? What is the function of "is" in the seemingly obvious statement "writing is read"?

## Reading Is Written

Like reading, writing entails a certain immediacy. In the moment of writing, one becomes a writer. I use "writer" here in a specific sense that is not to be confused with the notion of being a writer as a quality of an individual, as when someone who enjoys writing and writes a lot says, "I'm a writer." My interest here does not lie in the continual process of being a writer, but in the moment of writing when one becomes a writer. Deleuze and Guattari's concept of "incorporeal transformations," while not a concept they relate to writing, can shed light on this moment.

Like reading, writing is an incorporeal transformation. But all incorporeal transformations are not the same; while "writer" sensibly replaces "reader" in the above paragraph, which I cite from my earlier discussion of reading, one cannot say that the incorporeal transformations involved in becoming a writer are the same as those involved in becoming a reader. Incorporeal transformations share the characteristic of immediacy, but the effects each transformation produces vary widely. Becoming a reader is not the same as becoming a baseball player, or becoming a crowd. And even these transformations vary with each instance, as can be seen in the discussion of "I swear!" above.

With the differing qualities of incorporeal transformations in mind, I want now to ruminate over two key moments that compose the process of becoming a writer: the moment when words move from brain to page (e.g., the physical writing of words through a keyboard) and the moment these words are read by a reader.[2]

These days, most writing starts with a blinking cursor on a white screen. The endless disappearing and reappearing of the cursor serves as a constant reminder of the unrepeatable moments that compose writing. As one pauses in one's writing, the cursor disappears, returns, disappears, returns, and says "waiting, waiting, waiting, waiting." When your fingers hit the keys (with a momentary interval between each key hit), the cursor stops blinking, but the moment you stop, the blinking starts again. Writing happens in the intervals between blinking and unblinking, when the cursor is neither here nor there; in a sense the interminable blinking of the cursor serves as a marker of what Blanchot calls the "work's space," "the point at which here coincides with nowhere" (*Space* 48). For Blanchot, writing *is* the approach to this point: "To write is to find this point. No one writes who has not enabled language to maintain or provoke contact with this point" (48). Reaching this point is not, of course, as simple as firing up your word-processing program and beginning to write. No simple recipe for approaching this space exists.

Blanchot writes of the "essential solitude" that must be approached so that one can, in turn, inhabit the work's space. This solitude goes beyond the everyday understanding of solitude as "being alone" (Blanchot calls this "concentration"[21]) to a space where both the self and any conception of time become absent. In the work's space, "he who writes the work is set aside; he who has written it is dismissed" (21). This is the space of "the third person substituting for the 'I,'" of "myself become no one" (28), where "the 'I' that we are recognizes itself by sinking into the neutrality of a featureless third person" (30). Further, the writer himself or herself is never aware of the disappearance of the "I": "he who is dismissed does not know it" (21). Rather, the writer can only be "fascinated" by the negation of the "I" and can only affirm something that he or she cannot, by its very nature, comprehend. "What he is to write delivers the one who has to write to an affirmation over which he has no authority, which is itself without substance, which affirms nothing" (26). All of this is, Blanchot says, "interminable" and "incessant."

Likewise, the writer cannot understand or reflect on the absence of time in the work's space; he or she can only be fascinated by it. "To write is to surrender to the fascination of time's absence" (30). Such a surrendering is difficult to write about. Getting lost in the work—the experience of losing time, of sitting down to write at 9:00 a.m. and then suddenly realizing it is now 2:30 p.m.—is the only way to encounter time's absence, and of course this encounter only happens in retrospect when one asks, Where has the time gone?

Such reflection immediately removes one from the work's space. Recollecting this haunted space where everything is lost begins to hint at the essence of the work's space, where "'Everything has disappeared' appears" (253). After the "I" has been shed and time's absence has been surrendered to, an *apparition* appears, a haunting that says "precisely that when everything has disappeared, there still is something," (253) there still is the interminable murmuring of being. To become a writer entails not only hearing but also *silencing* this murmur.

> The one who writes is, as well, one who has "heard" the interminable and incessant, who has heard it as speech, has entered into this understanding with it, has lived with its demand, has

become lost in it and yet, in order to have sustained it, has necessarily made it stop—has, in this intermittence, rendered it perceptible, has proffered it by firmly reconciling it with this limit. He has mastered it by imposing measure. (37)

For Blanchot, one can only hear the interminable and incessant by turning away from it, by literally writing over it, by momentarily shouting it down. Kafka's writing "He was looking out his window" exemplifies the silencing of the interminable through which one writes. Writing the sentence creates an actuality from the virtual space of the interminable and the incessant, from the infinite murmur of the world. Kafka writes by subtracting from, or by limiting, the incessant murmur of being, so that all that is said is "He was looking out the window." In its actuality, the fact that it is written, this sentence silences everything else with "the certainty that what bursts into the light is none other than what was sleeping in the night" ("Literature" 305). From the apparition of the appearance of nothing this sentence appears. In the moment of writing the sentence, Kafka becomes a writer; he is "completely gathered up and enclosed in the sentence" ("Literature" 305). He has imposed measure on the infinite; as a writer he exists only in the space of this sentence. The existence of these words, in this order and called forth by the physical activities of Kafka's body, render him a writer.

At the same time, a second moment is integral here: that of the sentence being read. While Blanchot notes that a writer is "born" in the act of writing—"Let us suppose that the work has been written: with it the writer is born" ("Literature" 305)—he also notes that something else is necessary for a writer to become a writer. "He was looking out the window" makes Kafka a writer because he wrote it, but also because "it is a sentence that belongs to other people, people who can read it" ("Literature" 306). For writing to be readable, for Derrida's "writing is read" to be true, a written mark must be citable, as every written mark is.[3] The sentence must be able to move from the context in which Kafka wrote it, a context that the writer is "completely gathered up and enclosed in," to a space where the sentence can be read. For the sentence to be readable, it must *by necessity* be citable by Blanchot, by myself, and by any number of readers. It must be detachable from its origins. One need not know what Kafka meant by the sentence, or what the conditions of its creation were, in order to read it. Kafka's context *is not* a structural component of the mark, whereas the sentence's iterability, the possibility that others can read the sentence, *is* a structural component of the mark. That is, for writing to exist, it must be read. The "is" of Derrida's "writing is read" is an imperative; writing must be read, or it would not exist as writing. Likewise, Blanchot rhetorically asks, "What is a book no one reads? Something that is not yet written" (*Space* 193). Kafka becomes a writer in the instant of the citation of his sentence "He was looking out the window." Reading is, among other things, the citation of writing, which by necessity is citable, or readable.

## A Transformative Endeavor

The two moments involved in the creation of a writer show that the process is not linear but recurring; the process of becoming a writer is always beginning again. One becomes a writer in two interrelated moments, so that writing preexists reading (the moment of physically writing) and becoming a writer is an effect of reading (writing must be read). In other words, writing is an effect of reading, but also must preexist reading. A writer does not simply communicate information to a reader; a reader does not simply receive and interpret what has been written. With the imperative sense of "is" in mind, one can say, "Writing is read" and "Reading is written." And one can say this again and again, with infinite variations, with no origin or endpoint in sight. What is important here is that reading and writing are bound up in a process of continual variation. Kafka reads his own sentence and writes about it, Blanchot reads Kafka's writing about reading and writes about it, and I read Blanchot and write about it. I read Daitch rewriting (and thus reading) Kafka, and in my reading I write. And so on.

Reading and writing in such a manner is a transformative endeavor. Each moment of reading and writing functions as beginning without origin; the book is not a fixed and stable set of meanings waiting for a reader's interpretation. Rather, to read and write is, as Blanchot says, to "enter into complicity with the infinite variations of becoming" (*Space* 205). To read and write is to always remain open to the transformative power of the experience, to not attempt to finish a reading, and to say "this means that." The relation between reading and writing is much more complex than a conversation. "Reading is not a conversation; it does not discuss, it does not question. It never asks of the book, and still less of the author: 'What did you mean exactly? What truth, then, do you bring me?'" (194). This is not simply a question of the "death of the author" and his or her intentions. Reading and writing viewed as a process of continual variation makes it impossible even to ask these questions. Neither reader nor writer can lay claim to the truth of the text; both can only work to set limits on the text, not to simply say, "This can mean anything." To read a work is to define the limits of what that work can do, to "make perceptible" the effects produced by a reading. Reading is an act of affirmation, "an utterly joyful welcome to the work's generosity" (196). Reading activates the work and allows one to do something specific with a written work.

To say yes to the work is to enter into what Deleuze and Guattari call a "collective assemblage of enunciation" a grouping "of acts and statements, of incorporeal transformations attributed to bodies" (*Thousand* 88). Deleuze says that "literature is a collective assemblage of enunciation" ("Literature" 4), because the continual process of becoming a writer and of becoming a reader is produced by an assemblage constituted of the writer, the work, and the reader. To return to the discussion of baseball, the game itself gets produced through the collective assemblage of enunciation made up of the players on the field; the game is the enunciation, the effect of the incorporeal transformations that the players undergo in the recurring "one-thousandth[s] of a second" that make up the game. At the same time, baseball is not wholly and completely constituted by incorporeal transformations. Neither baseball nor literary criticism is cut off from the physical realities of the world: the bodies that play the game, the bodies that read and write. Reading and writing is not simply a daisy chain of texts. Something outside of literature prompts Kafka and Blanchot to write; something causes Susan Daitch to rewrite Kafka; something prompts me to write after reading, something beyond a desire to know what a text "means."

And this is where the role of literary criticism comes into play. Just as baseball player trains his body to play the game more effectively, a reader can train to increase his or her capacity to be affected by a text. Writing is not a one-way communicative street to reading; writers do not present the world to readers to be interpreted. Reading is not solving a puzzle. Reading is hearsay. Writing is read and taken somewhere else. The goal is not to get a handle on writing or even to produce more writing about another's writing. Rather, acts of reading and writing are transformative: I woke up to find myself transformed into a reader; I woke up to find myself transformed into a writer. If criticism—broadly defined as the act of writing about texts within an academic context—does any work here, it is to intensify one's capacity to be affected and to create continually differing spots of connection, not through knowledge, but through waiting, being prepared for the chance occurrence, and cultivating chance encounters. Criticism functions best as a catalyst, as a way of plugging into a reading and writing machine.

Reading and writing considered as a transformative endeavor changes the function of both activities, so that the communication of meaning is not the primary purpose of either. Writing, as a means of transformation, is not a means of understanding or describing the world. In "Literature and Life" Deleuze says that "to write is certainly not to impose a form (of expression) on the matter of lived experience. Literature rather moves in the direction of the ill-formed or the incomplete . . . Writing is a question of becoming, always incomplete, always in the midst of being formed . . . It is a process" (1). Writing does not transcribe the writer's lived experience; a written text does not serve as a touchstone of experience or as a fixed entity that gives an unchanging vantage point from which to understand the world. Writing becomes a process when considered as part of assemblage with reading, an assemblage that is always starting over, not defining but creating something anew, beginning again continually, with no origin or endpoint to rely on. A reader does not simply receive a written text but affirms the text's existence, and in this affirmation the reader takes the text someplace else, toward the creation of something new.

## "Killer Whales"

Susan Daitch and David Markson share a preoccupation with reading and writing; in this preoccupation, both writers show how the continual process of reading and writing takes part in the creation of a world and is a means of living in that world. The respective narrators of Daitch's "Killer Whales" and Markson's

*Wittgenstein's Mistress,* as well as the third-person voice of Markson's *Reader's Block,* employ reading and writing not as communication, but as a way of living in the world.

The narrator of "Killer Whales" does not do much more than read her world; in seven interrelated sections, the nameless narrator details the components of the world around her—her kitchen, the view out her kitchen window and into her neighbor's apartment, her job monitoring the language of sea mammals, the restaurant where she stops to eat—and employs various reading methods in her consideration of the world around her. All of these attempts at reading her world, through interpretation, mimesis, and scientific monitoring, fail to create meaning. None of these methodologies produces a means of understanding the connections that work to create the narrator's life. At the same time, "Killer Whales" is decidedly not a story of the failure of communication in late postmodern America. Daitch's story can be read as an affirmation of reading as a continual process, leading not toward resolution but toward, to repeat Blanchot's words, "enter[ing] into complicity with the infinite variations of becoming." The narrator of "Killer Whales" recognizes the impossibility of creating concrete meaning through reading; she gives up on trying to find an origin point from which the world will make sense. All the same, she goes on; she continues to relate to, and to configure, her world through reading.

As I argue above, starting with its first sentence, "Killer Whales" is a story concerned with reading. "I woke up to find Gregor Samsa in my sink" serves as a beginning, but not as an origin; this opening line serves as an entryway into the narrator's world, but not as a key for understanding that world. The citation of Gregor Samsa shows that the narrator uses reading as a means of connecting to the world: it is not a roach, but a literary character in the sink. At the same time, this citation does not lead to the easy conclusion that "Killer Whales" can be understood by the adjective "Kafkaesque." "Killer Whales" is not a story rife with references to Kafka; "Gregor Samsa" serves as a starting point, but this point does not lead toward a neat resolution in either plot or in interpretation. Rather, what links the sections of the story is the failure of reading to produce any meaning. The narrator does not develop her "Gregor Samsa" citation.[4] She covers the roach with a teacup, goes outside, and looks into her neighbor's window.

This view through his window frames the narrator's first failure of interpretation. Her neighbor sets up "tableaus" of figures
in his window.

> A statue of Saint Francis faced outward from the sill, arms out-
> stretched, one hand chipped off, white plaster showing through
> the scratched brown paint of his robe. He was surrounded by toy
> sheep, soldiers, a couple of windup Godzillas, a toy bed with two
> syringes in it, and a candlestick which had a flame-shaped light
> bulb where a wick would have been. (9–10)

No interpretation follows from the narrator's detailed description of this combination of objects. She notes only that "his
ground-floor apartment looked empty . . . the rooms were dim,
tables dusty" (10). A few pages later we learn that her neighbor
"is dying" (13); an attentive reader here might try to use this
information as a key for understanding the windowsill tableau
described earlier. But the narrator resists reading her neighbor's
tableau as a metaphor of death. She notes that her neighbor had
once set up a tableau involving fishbowls and Barbie dolls that
appeared to refer to the narrator's job of "annotating the speech
of sea animals" (11). She does not know what to make of this.
"I'm not sure if this was a gesture in my direction, a way of beck-
oning, teasing, or mimicking, and I never asked. Perhaps the
tableau had nothing to do with me at all" (12). And before the
fishbowl had appeared in the window,

> the sill had contained a collection of cigarette lighters shaped like
> pistols, and a lamp whose base was an Elvis Presley head. I'd
> thought my neighbor had an interest in things which model
> themselves after something else, which hide behind another his-
> tory, but now I'm not so sure. (13)

All of this detailed description serves only to frustrate interpretation. A week after the narrator describes the Saint Francis
tableau, the items are gone. "Objects have been removed from
his window, and it remained empty the next day as well" (16).
The sections of "Killer Whales" that detail the contents of the
neighbor's window evoke the kind of plot that often drives a
story—that is, death. But the neighbor's death is buried under
a focus on reading; plot—the narrator's relation to the neighbor, the cause of his death—becomes secondary to reading. The

narrator considers the neighbor's death as a matter of reading. "I don't know if there's been anyone in to learn his speech, anyone who could decode those window displays, and say with certainty, *this is what he meant by . . . and I will repeat to you . . .* I called him before I left, but no one picked up" (13; italics and ellipses in the original). In death, the certainty of communication fails. The meaning of the tableaus, as envisioned by the neighbor, dies with him. But reading continues. The narrator unreflectively shows that reading can never "say with certainty" what something means. Access to a concrete, final reading is always blocked; at the same time, such blockages are integral components of the very possibility of reading taking place.

The narrator's distance from her neighbor points to what Derrida calls "the possibility of disengagement and citational graft which belongs to the structure of every mark" ("Signature" 12). The tableaus can be separated from the neighbor's intention; the narrator can look through the window and read the arrangement of figures. In other words, the things that distance the narrator from her neighbor—the window, the unanswered phone, his death—or the spaces where communication breaks down are the same spaces that make a reading possible. Interpretation becomes impossible; the narrator cannot say that "this means that," and she cannot appeal to authorial intention to decode meaning. The unanswered phone—"no one picked up"—grounds the impossibility of finding an origin from which to produce an interpretation. There is no one who "can say with certainty" what the neighbor intended.

But the narrator still reads the tableaus. In a sense, her ability to say anything about the arrangements in the window shows that the possibility of reading and writing comes from its disengagement with an original meaning or intention. Derrida says that writing can be defined as "the possibility of its functioning being cut off, at a certain point, from its 'original' desire-to-say-what-one-means and from its participation in a saturable and constraining context" ("Signature" 12). While the original function of the neighbor's tableaus may have been to communicate to the narrator, the breakdown of this communication opens up the possibility of reading. The phone call and the act of looking through the window are primary here. Reading does not take place in the decoding of language, but in the call that the narrator makes, even because the call goes unanswered. The narrator responds to the tableaus in the window; she reads them and illustrates that reading need not offer a decoding or look for inherent connections or embedded meaning. The window tableaus do not mean anything. They illustrate that reading need have nothing to do with communication. The tableaus remain devoid of meaning, uninterpretable, but they lead the narrator, and perhaps the reader, toward a reconsideration of what it means to read. The narrator becomes a reader when she looks through the window, when she makes the phone call, when she acknowledges that she cannot decode the meaning of the window arrangements, when she cannot say, "This means that."

A two-paragraph section of "Killer Whales," which directly follows the narrator's first discussion of her neighbor's window, illustrates her changing thoughts on the function of language, and thus on reading and writing. For a time, the narrator says she thought that "words were like a school of jellyfish with thousands of tentacles streaming below the surface, and some of those tentacles were attached or stuck together below the waves" (10). Language refers only to itself and works through the connection of "syllables or synonyms" (10). Her search for these connections leads her to a search for the "origins" of language. She studies babies, "trying to determine when a child begins to . . . link the production of sounds to the expression of desire, gratification, or frustration" (10). After several years of such observation, she searches for the origins of language in "monkey chatter, and bird songs . . . [and] whale calls" (10). All of this leads her to conclude that words are "isolated catatonic patients" in "a scene of bankruptcy where there is no longer any relationship between sound and meaning" (11). All of her study leads her to become "even more convinced of the futility of this project, looking for sources" (11). She abandons her search for inherent connections and for origins, and she gives up this kind of search. But she does not quit her considerations of reading and writing.

Instead, she details how these failures begin to articulate an alternate way of engaging with the world. She begins to formulate an asignifying logic of fascination. A Greek restaurant she visits for coffee reminds her of Sam's, a diner she used to go to as a teenager. She calls up memories of a man getting arrested there and of "packages left in the phone booth" and "women [who] came and went in the late afternoon" (15). The narrator evokes a story, but remembers that, even at the time, she had no idea what was happening at Sam's. She recalls sitting in the diner: "I tried to listen to their conversations, but from the counter I couldn't really hear anything" (14). Her distance from events left her on the outside, trying to listen but unable to understand. Nonetheless, she kept returning to Sam's. She did not dwell in her failure to grasp the plot unfolding at Sam's. Rather, she dwelt in the fascination of listening, a fascination embodied by "an electric sign over the grill" (14) at Sam's.

> Above the name of the restaurant was a blackboard-colored field split by a hyperbolic curve with a dot of light tracing its trajectory. The spellbinding illusion was that the color of the dot of light changed as it traveled along the curve. Blue hill, green valley, yellow hill, red valley, purple hill, then back to the beginning, a visual metronome. It was mesmerizing when you had nothing to talk about, or even when you did. (14)

It is this fascination with the "mesmerizing" sign that remains a constant and links together the "failed" readings that the narrator describes. She remains fascinated, and this fascination becomes a way of life. The narrator's failed readings of her world become an affirmation of the impossibility of locating either an origin of meaning or a final meaning. But, in her fascination with reading the world, the narrator illustrates the impossibility of not reading. She cannot stop herself from reading and becoming mesmerized by the world. The narrator reconfigures reading as a continual process of becoming mesmerized over and over again, and of surrendering to this fascination and affirming that which is outside herself. Reading becomes an encounter with otherness.

Blanchot writes that "what fascinates us robs us of our power to give sense. It abandons its 'sensory' nature, abandons the world, draws back from the world, and draws us along. It no longer reveals itself to us, and yet if affirms itself in a presence foreign to the temporal present and to presence in space" (*Space* 32). Fascination, then, prevents interpretation of a certain kind. As the narrator remains mesmerized by the sign at Sam's, her desire to understand the actions of the diner's patrons diminishes to nothingness. Fascination is more than enough to bring her back again and again.

The power of this will-less fascination as a means of engaging otherness is illustrated most strongly in the narrator's job of "annotating [the] speech of" the killer whales that give the story its title. Her separation from the whales—by the monitoring equipment and the glass between the tank and the outside—makes the encounter possible. As with her other "failed" readings, the narrator does not produce meaning in her encounter with the whales. As she listens, she says "I was clueless" (12) to what the whales were saying. In watching and listening, she "recognize[s] patterns of sound, but the meanings they bark remain elusive" (17). In fact, the encounter is decidedly one-sided. The whales give "no sign" (11) of knowing she is there looking through the window. Yet she continues to "sit and watch" (17) "curves of whale speech snaking across a laboratory monitor" (17) late into the night. Reminded of the sign at Sam's, she surrenders to the fascination of reading. The story ends with the sentence "I am listening" (17). She is listening without hope of understanding. If the first sentence of "Killer Whales" creates identifiable readers, the last sentence both reaffirms this creation and begins to form a kind of logic for the readers created by the story. Through "Killer Whales," a reader becomes one who is listening. Listening to "Killer Whales" becomes an entryway into a reading and writing assemblage that makes no attempt to produce a meaning for or understanding of the story. "Killer Whales" trains me, as a reader, to forget interpretation as I attempt to cultivate a space of fascination in which I can read the story.

Reading "Killer Whales" alongside Blanchot, Derrida, and Deleuze helps me to cultivate just such a space of fascination, a space that puts me in proximity with the story's narrator. This narrator continues to read in the face of failed interpretation, and this is all that we, as readers, know about her. She reads the world around her and fails in a sense, but this failure points to a different strategy of engaging with the world. She reconfigures communication's breakdown as the beginning of reading. All of the blockages that prevent communication—her neighbor's window, the unanswered phone, the windows and monitoring equipment of the whale tanks, the distance that prevents hearing the other customers at Sam's—enable reading. Such blockages slow things down as they create an entryway into a space of Blanchotian fascination. The story resists mourning failed communication and instead works toward an ethics of reading that finds interpretation impossible, while at the same time finding giving up in futility to be equally impossible. Accounting for this refusal of both interpretation and silence becomes the work of an ethical literary criticism that must respond to, and be affected by, "Killer Whales's" constant fascination with the world. Literary criticism becomes an attempt both to surrender to the literary work's fascination and to articulate this surrender without recourse to interpretation.

## *Wittgenstein's Mistress*

David Markson's *Wittgenstein's Mistress* bears many similarities to "Killer Whales." Both feature first-person female narrators who present very little autobiographical material in their narratives. Narrative is not the primary concern of either text. I have discussed the plotlessness of "Killer Whales;" compared with *Wittgenstein's Mistress,* "Killer Whales" seems action-packed. Markson's novel consists of short (one- to two-sentence) paragraphs typed by the narrator, Kate. Through these paragraphs, the reader learns that Kate is the last person on earth.[5] Kate writes of her memories of her travels around the world that have led her to a house on a Long Island beach; in addition, some schematic, often contradictory, autobiographical information is presented. Joseph Tabbi, in his introduction to Markson's work, sees Kate's world as reduced to "the barest essentials: the house she lives in by the beach, the clothes she wears, or doesn't wear and puts out to dry, the books, the paintings and boxes that are stored in the house, remembered and (often as not) misremembered names, arcana, and anecdotal history" (Tabbi, "Solitary" 101).

Within this world of the barest essentials, Kate's narrative pays most attention not to matters of survival, as might be expected, but to writing and reading. Kate ruminates over the workings of her mind, what she calls "the baggage in one's head" (*Wittgenstein's* 72): memories of her own life, cultural ephemera, and questions about the way the mind forms connections. Kate often reflects on the writing process as the means by which connections are formed. "Many books frequently containing things that are connected to other things that one would have never expected them to be connected to" (104). A large part of *Wittgenstein's Mistress* consists of Kate's forging such connections. Kate links events in her own life to her memory of cultural artifacts. Sometimes these connections are prompted by the books in the house where Kate is living; other times the connections seem to come from nowhere. Often, Kate herself wonders how things get connected, as when she writes of one of her own sentences: "I am not quite certain how the second part of that sentence is connected to the beginning part, actually" (138). This detailed attention to reading and writing continues throughout the whole of *Wittgenstein's Mistress*. Kate never resolves her confusion, but she does not despair. She continues making connections and asking herself how and why she is making these connections.

Like the narrator of "Killer Whales," Kate reaches no conclusions; she never produces meanings in her writing. Yet, like the narrator of "Killer Whales," she continues on. Both narrators respond to the world by entering into a reading and writing assemblage. And most importantly, both can do nothing but respond. They constitute their voices as pure response to the world. The narrator of "Killer Whales" cannot make sense of the world, but she continues to read and listen. Kate continues to write, even as her writing does not lead toward understanding. A surrender to the transformative power of fascination characterizes both narrators. While the narrator of "Killer Whales" mostly reads, *Wittgenstein's Mistress* shows us that Kate writes. She writes in response to the world, "as if I have been appointed the curator of all the world" (227). The fleeting cultural references of "Killer Whales" do not compare to the dense weave of references in *Wittgenstein's Mistress*. The sheer number of cultural references in *Wittgenstein's Mistress*, and in Markson's more recent novels *Reader's Block* and *This Is Not a Novel* raise many questions for readers encountering them.

As I discuss above, a reader may or may not get the reference to Gregor Samsa that opens "Killer Whales." I argue that recognizing the reference to Kafka causes the reader to form certain connections, to be affected differently by the text. At the same time, missing the reference does not make the story impossible to read. "Killer Whales" contains only fleeting references to literature; in addition to Gregor Samsa, the name "Bartleby" and his famous phrase "I would prefer not to" pop up toward the end of the story. I will discuss the effects of the Bartleby reference below; my point here is that "Killer Whales" is not overly rife with literary allusions. While getting the references to Kafka and Melville renders distinguishable effects in a reader, not getting them does not prevent a reader from encountering the story. In fact, a mis- or nonrecognition could be said to be in line with the story's means of engaging the world and of continuing to read despite and because of missed connections. A reading that tries to interpret the references, to say that Gregor Samsa symbolizes this or that, may be more of a misreading than one that simply misses the reference altogether. All of this calls for an opening of the brackets I have earlier placed around misreading as a necessary prelude to any discussion of Markson's heavily allusive novels.

In "Limited Inc a b c," Jacques Derrida's reply to John Searle's (mis)reading of Derrida's "Signature Event Context" (which is in part a reading of J. L. Austin's *How to Do Things with Words*), Derrida cites Searle's characterization of Derrida's reading of Austin as "*more than simply a mis*reading" ("Limited" 41; italics in the original). I will not attempt here to untangle the finer points of the responses and counterresponses that take place (or do not take place, as Derrida says, "I don't know if it is quite taking place, if it ever will be able, or will have been able, quite, to take place; or if it does, between whom or what" [37]) between Derrida and Searle. Rather, I will cite Derrida's argument that the possibility of a misreading is a structural component of every mark. Regarding Searle, Derrida says, "The *mis* of those misunderstandings to which we have succumbed, or which each of us here accuses the other of having succumbed to, must have its essential condition of possibility in the structure of marks, of remarkable marks" (62). If a mark is to be read, it must be citable; the way in which a mark gets cited cannot be regulated before citation takes place. Every citation can easily be a miscitation; within every reading, the possibility of misreading exists inherently. In fact, reading and misreading cannot so easily be separated out from each other.

Derrida says that the functioning of a mark, that is, its ability to be cited and thus read, is not "in itself implying either that I *fully* understand what the other says, writes, meant to say or write, or even that he intended to say or write *in full* what remains to be read, or above all that any adequation need obtain between what he consciously intended, what he did, and what I do while 'reading'" ("Limited" 61). Nothing can guarantee that something read will be completely understood. A reader can know that Susan Daitch makes an allusion to Kafka; one can even say that Daitch intended to refer to Kafka. At the same time, a reader can never provide a full interpretation of Daitch's citation. Effects produced by Daitch's citation can be detailed, but a discussion of these effects can never provide a full context in which the function of the citation could be said to be understood. In other words, getting the allusion does not lead to mastery of "Killer Whales." If "I woke up to find Gregor Samsa in my sink" can be read, it must also always be re-citable, rereadable and recontextualizable. No reading can ever be a final reading. And this inability to produce a final reading, to fully understand what is being read, is not a failure of reading. It is reading's very possibility. Reading never stops responding. Reading's work is never done. Reading always remains open to a future encounter.

Why this lengthy digression on "missing"? Because, in *Wittgenstein's Mistress,* Kate's engagement with the world could be characterized in the same way that Searle characterizes Derrida's reading of Austin: as "more than simply a misreading." Kate's cultural citations are often confused. She writes that "Rainer Maria Raskolnikov" is a character in a novel by Dostoyevsky and that Anna Akhmatova is a character in *Anna Karenina;* she does not understand that the title of a book she comes across, *Baseball When the Grass Was Real,* refers to a time before the advent of Astroturf,[6] and she refers to the baseball player Stan Musial as "Stan Usual." She also has little familiarity with many of the writers she mentions, saying that she has not read a word of Nietszche and only a sentence of Wittgenstein; all that she knows of Heidegger is "that he was certainly partial to the word *Dasein*" (168). Even in the memories of her own past, Kate often contradicts herself; her son is referred to variously as Simon and Adam, and likewise her husband's name differs throughout her typings, as do the names of her lovers. Often, her personal life becomes confused with her cultural memories. She often writes about Helen of Troy, and in a remembered conversation with her mother, her mother calls Kate "Helen." Kate lists her lovers as "Simon or Vincent or Ludwig or Terry," (227) and a reader is left wondering if she is referring to Van Gogh, Wittgenstein, or men who just had the same first name.

All of these "misreadings" present a challenge to readers of *Wittgenstein's Mistress.* How does one react when Kate's misrecognitions are recognized? As Joseph Tabbi notes, Kate, self-appointed "curator of the world," is "a distinctly careless curator" ("Solitary" 756). How can the literary critic react to this "carelessness"? How does one respond to the "misses" that populate *Wittgenstein's Mistress*? Must critics take a step back and produce meanings to provide an order to Kate's rambling thoughts? Should the critic engage in corrective curating, becoming in a sense the curator of *Wittgenstein's Mistress*? Must readers strive for an understanding of Kate's references? Should they show that they know everything that Kate knows, and more, so that one recognizes both Kate's allusions and missed allusions? Must they get all of her references in order to respond to the novel?

Some critics at least hold out the possibility of getting all of Kate's allusions. In "The Empty Plenum: David Markson's *Wittgenstein's Mistress*," David Foster Wallace writes that "the novel's allusions are . . . a bitch to trace out . . . [which] makes a digestive reading of *WM* a challenging and protracted affair" (219). Of course, this raises the question of why one would want to trace out all of these allusions. In part, such a desire might stem from a reader's fear of missing something, of not understanding what Kate is typing, as Sherrill E. Grace points out in the first line of "Messages: Reading *Wittgenstein's Mistress*": "'In the beginning,' that is, on my first reading of David Markson's fourth novel, I knew I was missing many of the messages" (207). In a similar manner, some readers feel a desire to provide Kate with some of the connections she is missing. In the afterword to *Wittgenstein's Mistress*, Steven Moore writes that Kate "comes so close so often to making the link that the reader wants to shout it out at her as though in the audience of a game show" (247). Indeed, reading *Wittgenstein's Mistress* could easily turn into a game whose goal is to recognize all of Kate's allusions, and to point out and correct all of her errors.

Markson himself sees the recognition of his allusions as culturally important. He says, "I've always believed that it's a serious reader's responsibility to pick up on virtually any valid literary allusion—even though a shrewd novelist tries to bury such things too, of course, so that the context makes sense if the resonances are missed" (Tabbi, "Interview" 115). So, in a sense, for Markson, the serious reader must become a better curator than Kate. A serious reader should know everything that Kate (and Markson) knows. Missing allusions renders one a nonserious reader, a poor curator.[7] According to this way of reading, one gets less from one's reading experience if all allusions are not recognized.

But what, exactly, does one lose? Is a reader's capacity to be affected by *Wittgenstein's Mistress* lessened by an inability to get its allusions? Should missing allusions be characterized as a negative experience? Missing certain allusions does cause communication to breakdown, but as I argue above, the breakdown of communication opens up the possibility of reading. Reading *Wittgenstein's Mistress* as a corrective curator is to strive for communication, but it is also to attempt to render the novel a closed system, referring only to itself and the literary culture that all "serious" readers are already familiar with. As Wallace notes, such an attempt to understand all allusions is an attempt to communicate, but also to fold up into a solipsistic world. "The curator's job—to recall, choose, arrange: to impose order & only so communicate meaning—is marvelously synecdochic of the life of the solipsist, of the survival strategies apposite one's existence as monad in a world of diffracted fact" ("Empty" 226). To curate is to attempt to make sense and to reach a point where every cultural artifact can be cataloged, understood, and communicated. Kate never comes close to such a point in *Wittgenstein's Mistress*. And, of course, curating the whole of Western art is impossible. Any "curator of the world" is doomed to some sort of breakdown.

For some critics, this is precisely the point of *Wittgenstein's Mistress*. Kate will never be able to make every possible connection. Inevitably, she will miss something (and, of course, she misses a lot), and just as inevitably, her "mis" will function as a pointer toward a fundamental impossibility: loss, lack, death. Tabbi views Kate's fascination with the "cultural baggage" in her head as a means of avoiding thoughts of death, "as much a means of reflecting on life as needful means of blocking out thoughts of life's end" ("Solitary" 757). And to a certain extent Tabbi seems to be right on the mark. Kate does write about avoiding thoughts of death. But other readings seek to elevate the blocking out of thoughts of death and despair as the novel's central theme. Evelin E. Sullivan reads the last sentence of *Wittgenstein's Mistress*, "Someone is living on this beach," as "an echo of the first idea mentioned in the book, which, if pursued, would lead to the second idea, and to the third, and so on—to thoughts of loss and grief" (246). Likewise, in his afterword, Moore notes that "a sense of futility hangs over culture and history as Kate attempts to sort all this out, tempting the reader to equate Western civilization's greatest works of art and philosophy with the . . . messages she leaves in sand, washed away almost before she can complete them" (247). Such readings point to the impossibility of complete communication, of ever understanding and curating the entire world. While Kate fails in her project, her sacrifice serves to elevate culture. For Moore, the upshot of *Wittgenstein's Mistress* is that "civilization seems finally to have been worth it after all" (248). In turn, *Wittgenstein's Mistress* has become a part of the same Western canon. As Moore says, "I now couldn't become accustomed to a world without *Wittgenstein's Mistress*" (248). Likewise, Tabbi points to the "depth and cultural continuity" achieved in Markson's writing ("Introduction" 102). Getting the cultural references in *Wittgenstein's Mistress* seems to lead not toward an increase in a reader's capacity to be affected by the novel and to take it somewhere else, but rather toward an insular space that re-celebrates the centrality of Western culture, which now includes both *Wittgenstein's Mistress* and the critical reaction to it.

In this reading Kate becomes a solipsist who manages, through her failure as a curator, to reaffirm the centrality of culture. *Wittgenstein's Mistress* refers only to itself as it becomes a text taking its position at the end of the line of Western culture. It becomes a fiction about establishing the importance of the works Kate cites and miscites. The literary critic, in turn, recites the importance of the culture alluded to in the novel and places it within this tradition, with the result that *Wittgenstein's Mistress* becomes canonized as a great work of art in the Western tradition.

What are readers to do with what Markson calls "the very pulse and continuity of culture" ("Reviewers " 128) that is present in his allusive works? What can readers do with the myriad allusive connections formed in Markson's novels? What is left if one gives up on the impossible task of curating the whole world? How can one read *Wittgenstein's Mistress* as other than a mediation on loneliness and death? For some critics, and for Markson himself, the answer is simply to take pleasure in the ever-continuing forging of connections. Speaking of the fact that Wittgenstein and Hitler attended the same school at the same time, Markson writes, "Isn't that sort of thing just plain *fun* to be able to toy with?" ("Reviewers" 129). Tabbi picks up on this and celebrates the forging of connections that take place in Markson's novels. Tabbi places primary importance on this pleasure, at the expense of any consideration of the possible political effects of Markson's novels.

> Markson remains one of the most allusive of novelists, a writer who continues to demand from his readers a knowledge at least of the central modernist texts. He does this not out of any conservative desire for a return to classroom "standards"—Markson is not an academic or political novelist—but rather from a belief in the sheer pleasurability of creative recognition in the reading of literature. ("Solitary" 91)

I agree that Markson is not an outwardly "academic or political novelist"; at the same time, a tacit valorization of the Western canon can easily be read as one of the political effects of *Wittgenstein's Mistress* and other of Markson's works. My intention here is not to rehash canon politics; at the same time, it does seem important to note that "a belief in sheer pleasurability" can never be a simple or purely apolitical belief. Markson's writings do champion certain texts, and whether intentionally or not, such championing does have political import.

Canon politics aside, Tabbi's focus on the pleasure of recognizing Markson's allusions bears further consideration. This pleasure in recognition is also a pleasure in communication, a pleasure in community building. For Tabbi, Kate's logic of connectionism offers a new space of public "interaction and collaboration" that replaces the diminishing public squares and neighborhoods that "are becoming more and more rare in U.S. cities and towns" ("Solitary" 746). For Tabbi, the "ambitious" goal of *Wittgenstein's Mistress* is to create a "'virtual meeting space'" where authors and readers can be united. Reading *Wittgenstein's Mistress*, "readers in general might compare Markson's citational assemblage with the assemblage—the personal canon—that all readers carry in their head" (767). Again, readers can do this for the sheer pleasure of it; at the same time "the fun has a definite narrative function" (769). This function is the creation of a communication centered on a shared ground between writer and reader. Recognizing Markson's allusions, readers are reminded that we all carry an assemblage of texts in our heads; we can communicate through comparison, through "a solitary encounter uniting authors and readers" (769). Reading the novel allows one a momentary escape from "the media environment" (748) of the contemporary world; in reading, a reader can join the author in a "modest literary existence, refined down to a few books and works of music and visual art that for him [Markson] have persisted" (Tabbi, "Introduction " 102). In this space of collaboration, one can then reflect "on the power of ordinary language" ("Solitary" 749). Inhabiting this space, paying close attention to the connections Kate forges, "generates further narrative possibilities" (769) that can, in turn, forge new connections and create new spaces of communication between authors and readers.

But what if a reader cannot reach this space? What if readers do not join Tabbi in "enter[ing] sufficiently into Kate's solitude" (752)? What if readers miss the solitary encounter between author and reader for a more populous and noisy space, the space of the "mis-" itself? As I read and write around *Wittgenstein's Mistress,* the space around me is never purely mine. I blast my stereo, but I still hear the crushing noise of the construction site across the street; I hear the bass of my neighbor's stereo pulsating through my walls; images flicker in and out of my head; my personal canon is a disorganized, fluctuating mess beyond the help of any curator, let alone myself. Try as I might, I cannot get inside Kate's head; I can never enter into her solitude. The assemblage in my head constantly works its way outside; I cannot get close enough to it to order this assemblage, nor can I get far enough outside of it to grasp it in its entirety and compare it to the assemblage on the pages of *Wittgenstein's Mistress.*

I cannot communicate with Kate. I can read the last words of *Wittgenstein's Mistress,* "Someone is living on this beach," but I cannot agree with Sherrill Grace that when I finish the book, "Markson's Kate is waiting, still, time out of mind, for me to start reading again" (216). As a reader I can never communicate with the book and cannot provide an answer that Kate will hear; I can only read her message and offer a response that she will never receive. Still, like the narrator of "Killer Whales," I need not give up in light of the futility of failed communication. I can continue to read *Wittgenstein's Mistress* and reconfigure broken-down communication as an ethical response that shies away from understanding and connection and pays close attention to a continual series of misconnections. I can return to Derrida's question—"More than simply a mis-; what might that involve? Where will it lead us?" ("Signature" 41)—and begin to form an answer to it.

Where can Kate's "more than simply" misreadings lead a reader? Kate employs many strategies in her writing encounter with the world. In her failed attempts to act as the world's curator, she responds to the "cultural baggage" in her head in myriad ways. She remembers, forgets, imagines, reconfigures, ignores, denies, and tries to figure out. But she never tries to understand; she never catalogs in search of mastery. She follows her thoughts from here to there. She responds to the world and to her memory of the world. She cannot help but create new connections. She can never silence or completely order the assemblage in her head. But her thoughts continually lead her on. While they certainly do generate further narrative possibilities, Kate's (mis)connections point the way toward an ethics of response.

Her writings on the classics of art and literature rarely, if ever, attempt to understand or say what a certain text might mean. Her responses cannot be anticipated by the contents of the works she responds to. Kate shows that texts cannot contain their responses. A written work can only call for a response; it can never dictate what that response will be. Writing cannot demand that its call be answered as intended. The necessity of a response is a component of anything we call writing ("Writing is read"), but the characteristic of that response cannot be controlled. If I am to read (and write), I must respond, but my response can never be fully dictated. And my response irretrievably affects the "I" who is responding.

As Kate and the narrator of "Killer Whales" illustrate, the "I" who responds exists only in his or her response to the world. That is, neither narrator has any sort of interior life separate from her engagements with her world. In these engagements, both narrators move beyond the solipsism of the curator who seeks to order what is inside one's head so that it can be defined, centered, controlled, and thus communicated. Rather, both narrators continually negotiate between the interior spaces of their respective first-person voices and the exterior world that calls for a response. Their voices do not move from an interior "I" to an exterior world through a communication of consciousness; rather, both find their voices as they respond to the world, as they move within reading and writing assemblages and respond with fascination to the components of these assemblages. Both narrators show that to generate narrative is not to generate communication. Two examples can help illustrate the noncommunicative ways that the narrators read and write as they encounter the world: Kate's response to *Wuthering Heights* and an allusion to "Bartleby the Scrivener" in "Killer Whales."

Kate's brief writings on *Wuthering Heights* highlight an important component of her interactions with the world: looking out of windows. Her reading of *Wuthering Heights* is a response that has nothing to do with what the book might mean. Rather, she only recalls one aspect of the novel. "I do believe that I once read *Wuthering Heights,* however, which I mention because all that I seem to remember about it is that people are continually looking in or out of windows" (*Wittgenstein's* 53). Kate never develops this thought into a coherent interpretation of the novel[8]; rather, a fascination with windows becomes a continuing motif in *Wittgenstein's Mistress,* so that what Kate says about *Wuthering Heights* seems to describe *Wittgenstein's Mistress* also.[9] Indeed, Kate goes on to write that looking out windows is a component of life in general. "And life did go on. / Even if one sometimes appeared to spend much of it looking in and out windows" (226). Looking out windows is a way of engaging with the world.

Like the narrator of "Killer Whales," Kate surrenders to the fascination of a staring that never leads to understanding or meaning. For both narrators, looking out windows and staring at the world is a way of framing a call, not a means of self-validation. They cannot help but continually stare. Throughout *Wittgenstein's Mistress,* Kate is fascinated with a painting of the house she is living in, and particularly with a figure in the window of the painting. She writes, "As a matter of fact there also appears to be somebody at the very window [in the painting], upstairs, from which I watch the sunset. / I had not noticed her at all, before this. / If it is a she. The brushwork is fairly abstract, at that point, so there is little more than a hint of anybody, really" (40). Kate never resolves her confusion; she reaches no conclusion about the figure in the painting's window. Tabbi diagnoses this unresolved fascination as solipsism, "a near total lack of interest" ("Solitary" 766) in the outside world and in "empirical verification" (766). In this reading of Kate as solipsistic, her fascination points to a turning inward, a self-validation that Kate fails to recognize but that readers will notice. "To readers (though not to Kate) the woman in the painting is obviously a projection of herself—indeed, it's altogether possible that she was the painter. But Kate is bewitched by her own language and transfixed by the returning stare of her own gaze" (766). While it is certainly possible that Kate painted the picture, it seems unclear how her fascination with the painting functions as a mirror stage of self-identification. Kate is bewitched, not by her own gaze, but by the resistance of the object she stares at. The figure in the painting never resolves into a reflection; it never resolves into anything more distinct than a "fairly abstract" brushstroke. Kate stares out at the world, but she never reduces what is outside her to what is in her head. She never sees herself reflected in the world; rather, her voice (which is her whole existence for readers) is constituted in her response to the world, in her rambling, indecisive, and nonconclusive ruminations on the figure in the painting. Her fascination with the painting is reminiscent of the "Killer Whales" narrator's fascination with the electric sign in the diner—"[It] was mesmerizing when you had nothing to talk about, or even when you did" (14)—that likewise produces no self-validation or other meaning.

What Tabbi characterizes as solipsism—staring to the point of complete self-involvement—is a way out of Kate's head, for her and the reader, to a connection to the world that is not communicative, to a fascination that reconfigures thought. Looking out a window, staring in fascination, is not curating or understanding; it does not reduce the otherness of the world to that of interior thought. Staring—fascination—is a way of responding that has nothing to do with mastery. Looking out a window is a movement toward the outside that responds without erasing the difference between self and other.

This noncommunicative space of fascination is not a utopian space where one can simply say, "I am ethical because I respect the otherness of the world." For Kate and the narrator of "Killer Whales," fascination is characterized by the absence of any choice. They do not choose to surrender to the mesmerizing world around them; they have no choice but to continue to respond. For both of them, life equals response. When Kate says that "in either event people continually looking in and out of windows is doubtless not such a ridiculous subject for a book, after all" (134), she is saying, in effect, that life is not such a ridiculous subject for a book.

Kate links writing and a fascination with looking out windows so strongly that *Wittgenstein's Mistress* becomes a book whose subject is "people continually looking in and out of windows." She does not write to order her life; she does not write out of grief, loss, or loneliness, or because she is a solipsist; she does not write in order to generate further narrative possibilities. After brief consideration, over the course of a few pages toward the end of *Wittgenstein's Mistress,* she rejects the very notion of auto-biography. "Quite possibly I might have to start right from the beginning and write something different altogether. / Such as a novel, say" (229). She then wonders if "it just might change matters if I were to make it an absolutely autobiographical novel?" (230). This question generates many conjectures that lead Kate to write, "Doubtless making it just as well that writing novels is not my trade in either case" (232). She abandons the idea of a novel, writing that "it was at least seven or eight weeks ago" (233) since she had considered the idea.

Kate's writing becomes autobiographical, not in the sense that she is writing her life story, but in the sense that she is writing herself into existence. Through writing, she singularizes her voice out of the baggage in her head. She creates what Deleuze calls "a zone of proximity" with the thoughts in her head. For Deleuze, the creation of such a zone of proximity is the primary effect of writing. To write "is not to attain a form (identification, imitation, mimesis) but to find the zone of proximity . . . singu-larized out of a population rather than determined in a form" ("Literature" 1–2). Kate's writing connects her to the only pop-ulation that exists in her world: the "cultural baggage" in her head. Her only means of forming a zone of proximity with this baggage is through writing, through creating a voice by sub-tracting herself from the totality of her mind. She never seeks to present these subtractions as a coherent whole; she constantly returns to previous thoughts and rewrites them; she often forgets what she has already written; she contradicts herself; her goal is not a logic of connections. She never strives toward a linear, coherent narrative. All of these constant returns show that Kate's writing herself into life is a continual process of variation; from page to page, she becomes a writer again and again, every time she begins to type.

Just as Kate writes herself into existence, so the narrator of "Killer Whales" reads herself into existence. Like Kate writing, the "Killer Whales" narrator does not continually read in order to form a logic of connections, nor does she read to generate further narrative possibilities. In fact, she never considers the possibility of not reading. Her continuing fascination with the world never appears as something chosen. She cannot help but read. At the same time, her reading of the world around her is never all-encompassing. She never claims an understanding of others. She never interprets the tableaus in her neighbor's window. And later in the story, at a restaurant named Demeter's near where she works, she again notes that reading does not lead toward understanding.

In the restaurant she hears news of the Persian Gulf war on the radio. "*Tariq, Kerkuk, Baghdad, Mesopotamia,* and *Al Basra* slam into *typhus, typhoid, microorganisms* . . . I try to imitate the announcer but am unable to mimic his speech" (ellipses in original, 16). Mimesis fails. The narrator listens further in fascination. "*Forty thousand body bags have just been ordered, although no shot has yet been fired*" (16). She thinks of the people making these body bags and thinks of Bartleby: "If Bartleby suffered paralysis as a result of working in a dead letter office, those who sew and measure zippers and nylon on a body bag assembly line may also linger in future cells saying only *I prefer not to*. No one will guess their histories" (16). Missing the allusion to Melville's "Bartleby the Scrivener" might produce a failure of recognition similar to the one the narrator notes. Getting the allusion can produce more distinct effects.

Bartleby, in his endless repetitions of the phrase "I would prefer not to," embodies what Deleuze calls "the growth of a nothingness of the will . . . Pure patient passivity, as Blanchot would say" ("Bartleby" 71). This passivity creates a zone of proximity among Bartleby, the narrator of "Killer Whales," and Kate. All three, to a certain degree, manifest this "nothingness of the will" as they variously surrender to the fascination of Bartleby's statement "I would prefer not to be a little reasonable" (qtd. in Deleuze 69). Kate and the narrator of "Killer Whales" become close to Bartleby in their continuing responses to the world—through writing and reading, respectively—that constantly flee meaning, understanding, or explanation, and dwell in fascination. Bartleby never explains his reasons for preferring not to do anything. Such explanations would only interrupt his "pure patient passivity." The narrator of "Killer Whales" never explains why she continues to read, to listen, even as she produces no understanding of the things she reads. Just as for Bartleby, such explanations would only interrupt her cultivation of fascination. Likewise, Kate never offers conclusive reasons for writing; she never attributes a meaning to what she writes, and she produces no understanding of the baggage in her head. This "nothingness of the will" supplants any will for generating narratives or creating connections. At the same time, Bartleby's passivity far exceeds that of both Kate and the "Killer Whales" narrator. While the response to Bartleby's passivity leads to his eventual death, Kate and the narrator employ their will to nothingness only in the face of meaning and interpretation. While they bring to a stop the types of writing and reading that produce meanings, they continue to engage with the world through the very acts of reading and writing. Bartleby, of course, proceeds only through a continuing series of "I would prefer not to" that places him at a remove from the whole world and moves him closer and closer to death. In her somewhat lesser passivity (that is, she never goes so far, as Bartleby does, as preferring not to eat), the narrator of "Killer Whales" shares a commonality with the attorney who narrates "Bartleby" and is both attracted and repelled by Bartleby's passivity.

In the final paragraphs of Bartleby, the attorney says he is "unable to gratify" (Melville 34) any desire to know Bartleby's history, just as the narrator of "Killer Whales" notes the impossibility of guessing the history of the people who manufacture body bags. At the same time, the attorney ends on a much less outward note than "I am listening." As he reflects on Bartleby's death, the attorney proclaims, "Ah, Bartleby! Ah, humanity!" (Melville 35). Deleuze claims that this "does not indicate a connection, but rather an alternative in which he has had to choose the all-too-human law over Bartleby" ("Bartleby" 81). The attorney cannot surrender to his fascination with Bartleby; indeed, in the face of "I would prefer not to," the attorney flees Bartleby, "dodging everyone by the suddenness and rapidity of my flight" (Melville 30). This flight leads the attorney away from fascination, away from Bartleby's logic of preferences, away from his preference not to be reasonable. The attorney's flight leads directly to Bartleby's arrest and subsequent death. In choosing the "all-too-human law," the narrator runs toward meaning, toward reason, and condemns Bartleby to arrest.

At the same time, the narrator's exclamation ("Ah!") becomes a sign of not choosing, becomes an involuntary fascination with Bartleby, and becomes a sign that the narrator has been affected by Bartleby. In the impossibility of not rendering Bartleby the subject of the law, the exclamation is not on purpose, or is purposeless; it is a sign of fascination, of remembrance, and of an involuntary response to Bartleby. The narrator flees, but in his fleeing he gestures toward another, impossible order: the choosing of Bartleby over the all-too-human choice of the law and "Humanity." How could this inhuman choice be rendered? How could the narrator, a successful attorney, move toward a Bartleby-like nothingness of the will? He would have to get another job, perhaps monitoring killer whales.

While the narrator of "Killer Whales" shares the attorney's fascination with Bartleby, she never moves toward the pole of humanity. In her continuing process of reading, the narrator affirms Bartleby; she affirms the nothingness of the will that has nothing to do with the process of creating meaning. Likewise, as she continues writing without will, Kate moves away from humanity, from the desire to act as the world's curator and toward an engagement with the baggage in her head that never moves toward reason, order, or significance.

To choose Bartleby, to surrender to fascination, is to affirm the reading and writing assemblage as noncommunicative, as a response to an other that does not reduce to the same and that does not merely increase narrative possibilities. To surrender to fascination is to enter a reading and writing machine without a prefigured goal of saying what something means. Kate and the narrator of "Killer Whales" proceed by their various logics of fascination to create noncommunicative ways of living in the world. They never explain themselves; they never offer reasons for their continuing to write and read. Deleuze argues that such logics are characteristic of American literature. He writes that "the founding act of the American novel . . . was to take the novel far from the order of reasons, and to give birth to characters who exist in nothingness, survive only in the void, defy logic and psychology and keep their mystery until the end ("Bartleby" 81). "Killer Whales" and *Wittgenstein's Mistress* never provide psychological depth or motivations for their characters. At the same time, through their responses, these characters achieve a singularity that refuses categorization as either cipher or as "everywoman" with whom a reader can identify. Kate and the narrator are constituted purely as they respond to the world. They do not preexist their acts of writing and reading, and they never conclude these acts.

Putting the last lines of *Wittgenstein's Mistress* and "Killer Whales" in proximity leads toward the creation of a continual, non-communicative reading/writing assemblage. "Someone is living on this beach." "I am listening." These final two sentences function not as a communication, but as a continual echo, repeating and repeating, not answering one another but showing that reading and writing are both always moving towards an outside, and away from an interior spaces of communication. To write is to say "Someone is living on this beach;" to read is to say "I am listening." To continue to read and write is not to despair that the two sentences will never communicate. To read and write is to respond to the otherness of the world, to surrender to the oscillations between the inside and outside of a reading/writing machine. Reading and writing are not machines geared to generate more and more narrative possibilities; reading and writing are an assemblage constituted by response. Reading and writing build a machine producing nothing but enunciations, nothing but ways of living.

# CHAPTER 2

# FASCINATED DISGUST IN RICHARD POWERS

*Who gives? What is given?*

　　—*Maurice Blanchot*, The Writing of the Disaster *(110)*

I want to say nothing about Richard Powers. But some force compels me to write. So I start in Powers's *Gold Bug Variations*, with Stuart Ressler riding a Greyhound to a postdoctoral appointment at the University of Illinois. Just outside his destination,

> a stream of tortoises possessed of mass migratory instinct crawl over the highway in the twilight. Bottlenecked cars take turns gunning, crunching over the shells. The tortoise-trickle does not even waver. Ressler stares out the window as long as he can stomach it. For a hundred yards, he can make out the horror. The insane persistence of the parade holds him in fascinated disgust. (44)

Why start, from among the thousands of pages of fiction written by Powers, with this scene of carnage? The "fascinated disgust" that holds Ressler spellbound to the tortoises' procession articulates a concern that resonates through all of Powers's work. Ressler's inability to turn away mirrors the inability of the tortoises to stop their "parade"; it mirrors the inability of the traffic to not progress toward its destination; it mirrors the impossibility of not building the highway that the traffic cannot help but drive on. Ressler's "fascinated disgust" describes a double-edged desire—to quit and to go on, to stop and to progress—that possesses both Powers's characters and his narrative voice.

This fascinated disgust recurs under many guises throughout all of Powers's novels, but is often overlooked or only partially considered in the data stream of information that flows around the novels. For instance, two of Powers's best critics, Tom LeClair and

Joseph Tabbi, write of either fascination or disgust, but never both. LeClair, in "The Prodigious Fiction of Richard Powers, William Vollman, and David Foster Wallace," writes of the fascination, or "excited amazement and wonder" (16), of Powers's novels. Joseph Tabbi configures the "disgust" that flows through Powers's novels as a desire to quit that must be overcome.

LeClair argues that Powers, Vollman, and Wallace write with "amazement at the natural world they depict circulating through us and buzzing around us, wonder at the intricate and dense fictions they offer as imitative forms of that world" (16). This amazement and wonder on the part of the author can be communicated to readers through "the emotional effect of realistic representation" (24). That is, Powers transfers his fascination with the world to the reader, via his "intricate and dense fictions." The act of reading Powers builds "toward the final response of wonder, the reader's amazement at the world created in and through this book made by an author 'giving or yielding abundantly'" (24). Fascination is a gift given by authors to readers. The communication of wonder that connects writers and readers works through a representation of the world, "as the authors warn against mankind's leaving the course of nature and becoming a monster in the world web of life, destroying itself in the process . . . creators, created, and audience are all braided together" (16–17). This understanding of fascination does not account for the involuntary nature of wonder being thrust upon a reader by "an author 'giving or yielding abundantly.'" That is, the tortoises in the above citation could easily be said to be "giving or yielding abundantly" to the flow of traffic, to Ressler's eyes, and to a reader's sense of wonder. Fascination here is irretrievably paired with disgust. In this pairing, a reader does not simply receive an author's gift of amazement; fascinated disgust produces not communicative splendor or wonder, but an inability to look away from "horror." The braiding together that LeClair speaks of can be seen as a kind of monstrous complicity, a connection neither asked for nor necessarily desired.

Conversely, Joseph Tabbi focuses on the "disgust" manifested by many of Powers's characters, while paying little attention to how this disgust is linked with fascination. Tabbi notes that "too many of Powers' main characters have the air of a prodigy who is proudly called on by adults to trot out what she has learned. And yet, when his characters do light on a research quest of real interest, they dread completion of their search" ("Fiction" par. 24). This "dread" recurs throughout Powers' work as a sort of giving up, shown in

> the moment when his main character, like Ressler, ceases to fill the world with *content* and instead steps outside the frame. That's when Adie Klarpol erases the files (but for one set) that she had once used to fill a virtual reality "Cavern" with canonical art; it's what causes "Helen," an Artificial Intelligence, to self-destruct when she is given the worldly context for the canonical literature she's been made to memorize. In every case, the backlash is as total as the naiveté with which the educational process is undertaken. (par. 19)

All of these characters abandon their research quests in disgust at their inability to achieve "godlike knowledge outside of social, military, and commercial constraints" (par. 19). For Tabbi, Powers's characters quit when they realize that transcendence always fails, that, as Tabbi quotes from Powers's *Galatea 2.2,* "'understanding can never be large enough to include itself' (315)" (par. 21). Tabbi sees this inability to achieve "internal distancing" (par. 22) as a continuing struggle in Powers's work. Tabbi writes that Powers "has generally been less successful . . . in creating, in his characters, a 'faculty of mind' that would allow them to" (par. 24) achieve this distancing.

Still, Tabbi notes that a watershed moment occurs in *Galatea 2.2* when Powers narrates his own writer's block. For Tabbi, "even the presentation of blockage, surely the most private of the writerly experiences, represents one writer's attempt . . . to go on working in a medium that is newly conscious of itself as such" (par. 29). Self-reflection thus becomes a representational strategy for overcoming the inability to transcend the self. The very "presentation of blockage" situates it not as a personal matter of the subjective self, but as part of "a cultural production" (par. 29). Tabbi is not arguing that Powers's self-reflexivity is a kind of "belated modernist reflexivity" (par. 29). Rather, the representation of writer's block in Powers begins "to dissolve the unity and all-too-complete knowledge that he had patiently accumulated . . . up to that point" (par. 24). The author cannot stand apart from the cognitive networks that inform his or her text; furthermore, Tabbi argues, writers need to be aware of "the condition of consciousness, which is always belated and to the side of itself" (par. 29). For Tabbi, what Powers realizes is that consciousness can never be fully experienced or expressed, because the act of writing is always a material, cultural practice. Self-consciousness is not enough. Tabbi calls for a situated awareness of self-consciousness. "To overcome this widespread cultural blockage, a rearrangement or recomposition of the relations among communicating media is needed, so that meaningful communication can again course through the reconfigured hardware of a newly constructed discourse network" (par. 29). For communication to take place in the contemporary, cognitive world, the dread and disgust felt by Powers's characters needs to be overcome twice: first personally, by understanding that full self-consciousness is impossible, and then culturally, by understanding that even self-consciousness depends on the material practice of discourse networks.

Tabbi seems right that the most interesting of today's contemporary writers write with a more than metafictional awareness of the practice of crafting fiction. At the same time, both Tabbi and LeClair assume that communication and representation are the ultimate goals of contemporary fiction. For LeClair, as noted above, "creators, created, and audience are all braided together" (17) by the density of contemporary writers such as Powers. Tabbi envisions similar connections being forged by contemporary writing practices. "The author himself, looking at what he has done, is only another 'Reader,' who must collectively cognize the completed work and carry it forward, as a block of experience, into a new discourse network of reading, writing and publishing" ("Fiction" par. 29). While LeClair and Tabbi take different angles, for both, fascination and disgust work as pathways to greater communication, as we move into "the complexities of a cognitive age" (Tabbi, "Fiction" par. 32). But what if fascination and disgust are not intrinsically linked with communication, or even with cognition?

That is, instead of assuming that fascination and disgust ultimately engender communication, I want to slow down and ask precisely how fascinated disgust functions in Powers. In *Kafka*, Deleuze and Guattari write that "it is absolutely useless to look for a theme in a writer if one hasn't asked exactly what its importance is in the work—that is, *how it functions* (and not what its 'sense' is)" (45). In other words, noting that fascinated disgust recurs throughout Powers's fiction is only a first step. The function of fascinated disgust—that is, what it does both in the novels and to readers—must be considered, because, as Powers writes in *Galatea 2.2*, "the point of stories was what you did with them" (108). In a similar way, one can say that the point of fascinated disgust is what you do with it, and what it does to you. Fascinated disgust certainly functions as a connective force throughout Powers, but these connections do not necessarily serve communication through the production of awe, nor are they necessarily states to be worked through and overcome. Fascinated disgust often blocks communication in Powers's novels, and this blockage calls for a critical engagement that necessitates examining some of the literary-critical assumptions regarding communication and subjectivity.

In the "new discourse network of reading, writing and publishing" that Tabbi calls for, the relation between reading and writing may need reconfiguration. Literary theory and criticism can prove helpful here. Powers's work shows a strong awareness of literary criticism. In an interview he says that he refuses to see "the revolution in critical theory as a war against the literary artifact" (J. Williams 5). Instead, he says, "I've worked to understand the challenge of theory, and to see these new ideas not as threats to my role as a cultural producer but as a call to greater levels of writerly accountability" (5). In *Gain*, he says that he tried "to be very aware of deconstruction and poststructuralism and to incorporate those notions into the story it tells" (5). In other words, in Powers's fiction, the connection between literary criticism and literature grows complex in a way that undermines any straight lines of communication between a novel and a reader. On returning after many years to the university where he had studied, "Richard Powers," the narrator of Powers's *Galatea 2.2*, notes that "criticism had gotten more involuted while I was away. The author was dead, the text-function a plot to preserve illicit privilege, and meaning an ambiguous social construction of no more than sardonic interest" (191). This hyperawareness of critical theory demands a close look at the function of reading. Reading functions differently when the texts being read are hypersensitive to their being read and theorized over. The borders between text, author, and reader become blurred. In a conversation with a student, "Powers" speaks of the "common core of humanity" and is told, "And you wonder why the posthumanists reduced your type to an author function" (286). The constant doublings of Powers's fiction create ever-varying circuits that frustrate attempts at understanding. It becomes difficult, if not impossible, to pull a theme or idea such as fascinated disgust out of Powers and say what it means. Considering how fascinated disgust functions draws the reader into a reflexive relation with fascinated disgust. That is, as I argue above, it functions in Powers to both draw and repulse characters. In a sense, it can connect to a reader in a similar way: as I write about it, the concept reworks my connection to what I am reading and writing about. Fascinated disgust cannot be examined or have light shed on it so easily; it is more of a continuing fluctuation that cannot be measured or pinned down, but can only be encountered through singular acts of reading.

Nothing about these acts of reading is inherently communicative. Rather, reading Powers calls into question the nature of the reading and writing "selves" assumed as nodes of a communicating network. Powers claims that "books should not flatter our sense of self. They should interrogate it" (Morrow and Powers 4). Such an interrogation can work both within a text and on a reader. Powers's novels interrogate what counts as a "self" in fiction, and they interrogate what kind of "self" can respond to his fiction. "We can learn to read in a way that sees extended acts of narrative or even discursive prose as 'characters'—sometimes ironized, sometimes frail or faulty, but always living, voiced depictions in their own right" (7). What Tabbi calls "the increasing hopelessness of [Powers's] first four books" ("Fiction" par. 19) is not an attitude to be overcome. Rather, this "hopelessness" is a "character," a "living" emergent subjectivity that demands that readers learn to read anew. The fascinated disgust that runs through Powers's novels can be instructive here.

Fascinated disgust resonates through all of Powers's novels, as both character—the father Eddie Hobson in *Prisoner's Dilemma*, the aforementioned Ressler in *The Gold Bug Variations*, Helen, the computer, in *Galatea 2.2*, Benjamin Clare in *Gain*, and the artist Adie Klarpol in *Plowing the Dark*—and "extended acts of narrative," a tone and style that permeates the novels. In addition, fascinated disgust can be viewed as a force that might possess readers of Powers, so that they continue through long discursive passages and detailed tangents, unable to turn away. In a sense, fascinated disgust functions as a life force throughout Powers's work, animating both the "living, voiced depictions" of his prose and the readers of that prose. Perhaps the greatest challenge of reading Powers lies in formulating a way of reading that does not rest on communicative assumptions, that does not assume that a reader can simply understand the emergent subjectivities produced by and in Powers's fiction. In other words, reading Powers calls out for close consideration of the function of fascinated disgust before assuming any sort of "meaningful communication" as a goal, before being sure that there even is a goal.

## The Use of Use

Working in a goalless space brings one into the realm of what Powers' calls the "use of use," a theme that arises in a discursive passage in *The Gold Bug Variations* that describes Christmas week.

> Briefly humanity recalls, in a dream of distant past, that use is no use. For a week, it's again clear that the question is not ends and applications, but shape, sound, angels arriving on the raw doorstep, an ache, an instant hint, singing the new year in, in a bleak midwinter. Then back to grim progress. (414)

The claim that "use is no use" raises important questions when considered as an interrogation of the novels themselves. Why write them? Why read them? What's the use of fiction? In other words, even as I begin to map out the subjectivities that emerge in and around Powers's fiction, I am confronted by questions about the use of this mapping. For instance, what's the use of mapping the function of fascinated disgust?

* * *

In *The Writing of the Disaster,* Maurice Blanchot claims that "writing, since it persists in a relation of irregularity with itself—and thus with the utterly other—does not know what will become of it politically: this is its intransitivity, its necessarily indirect relation to the political" (78). The political—I understand the political here in the sense Powers uses: "politics is psychology as it plays out in groups larger than two" (J. Williams 12)—use(s) of fiction cannot be easily determined, because fiction does not directly relate to an object. A work of fiction, for Blanchot, cannot function as a direct political action planned by an author; rather, the use that writing will be put to—a work of fiction's place in the world—remains to be determined. Criticism has a role to play in this determination, but at the same time criticism has a certain intransitivity, a goallessness, itself. Blanchot calls for "patience" in producing criticism. "Criticism is almost always important, even if it omits and misrepresents a great deal. However, when straight-away, it becomes warlike, this is because political impatience has won out over the patience proper to the 'poetic'" (*Writing* 78). It is important to note here that Blanchot forges a link between writing, criticism, the "poetic," and the political, as he is too often read as a purely textual critic with no interest in the political use of fiction.[1] Blanchot's proper "patience" can be compared to Powers's claim that "use is no use." Both call for a slowing down of processes, a kind of halting that moves tentatively and indirectly. Criticism becomes an integral part of this halting, a slowing down of the reading process that moves away from the goal of communication.[2]

A goalless criticism locates fiction in a space where use is of no immediate use, but where the unforeseeable connections between reading, writing, and the world get produced. Paying close attention to these connections leads to the political use of fiction, a use that can only be known as it emerges from the singular encounter between readers and texts. A passage from *Gain* illustrates the unexpected connections that can be forged by reading. Laura Bodey's son is struggling through a homework assignment of reading Whitman's "Crossing Brooklyn Ferry." Seeing that he is struggling, she asks, "What are you supposed to do with it?" (86) to which he replies, "Supposed to say what it's fucking about" (86). Laura struggles with her son to find an answer. "She tries to read faster. But the faster she goes, the less she gets" (87). Her son's impatience prevents a slowing down of the reading process, and Laura decides that "she will tell her kid all the wrong answers. Hopelessly muddle these lines for him, forever . . . But she will at least sit down with him now, today, while sitting is still possible, until the verse is done" (88). Even as it is read quickly, the poem creates a brief pocket of space where nothing gets produced. Laura produces a few readings that relate the poem to communication: "He's trying to talk with everyone who is ever going to be taking this boat . . . People fifty years later" (88); "He's trying to imagine . . . all these lives" (88, ellipses in the original). But her interpretation is stopped dead by her son's response: "Why?" (88). They give up their reading.

But this failed struggle for interpretation, for saying, "What it's fucking about," points to the difficulty of reading as a search for meaning. Deleuze makes a distinction between interpretation and experimentation in reading. Interpretation cuts off the text from the world and only refers back to the text; to say what something means is to say either that "the work is supposed to find its end in itself" (Deleuze and Parnet 49) or that it is a simple one-to-one representation of the world, that "this means that." Reading, as a form of experimentation, or what Deleuze calls "programs of life" (48), is "a means of providing reference points for an experiment which exceeds our capacity to foresee" (48). Reading cannot know what will become of it. Such a goalless form of reading proves more immediately difficult than saying what something means. For Laura, reading Whitman's poem is "like doing some kind of Martian archaeology" (*Gain* 87). Reading is an encounter with otherness, where the rules of, or even the reason for, the encounter are not given, but must be produced. Reading continually interrogates not just "why" but also "how" we read, as it produces unforeseen connections and leads in unexpected directions.

The lines of "Crossing Brooklyn Ferry" cited in *Gain* give further valence to these questions and begin to push them into the realm of ethics, into the realm where one must continually ask why and how otherness gets encountered. "*We use you, you objects, and do not cast you aside—we plant you permanently within us, We fathom you not—we love you . . . You furnish your part towards eternity*" (89, italics and ellipses in the original). If encounters with the world are a matter of use ("we use you, you objects"), they are also something more ("we plant you permanently within us"). The connections "we" form with the "objects" of the world go beyond use value and into the production of something unforeseeable, something perhaps dangerous. Powers's citation of these lines resonates with Laura's cancer, perhaps the result of her encounter with the products produced by Clare, that she now carries within herself. Looking through her house, Laura sees Clare products everywhere. "The house is full of them . . . . They perch on her microwave, camp out at her stove, hang from her shower head. Clare hiding under the sink, swarming her medicine chest, lining the shelves in her basement, parked out in the garage, piled up in the shed" (304). She knows that this encounter with objects is beyond choice, that "she brought them in, by choice, toted them in a shopping bag. And she'd do it all over again, given the choice. Would have to" (304). In other words, her choice to bring these products into her home is an effect of a whole system of marketing and selling that is beyond her control. And the result of her choice entails an incorporation—a bodily relation with these products that may have caused her cancer—that is not subject to any kind of choice. Living is an encounter with otherness; lack of choice prevents "why" questions from being asked. Reading Powers's novels raises questions about the political and ethical implications of how one encounters the world. How do we respond to objects, to otherness, when we have no choice but to respond? Can otherness be considered outside the realm of use? With these questions in mind, I turn to a character from *Gain* who is thoroughly animated by a fascinated disgust that spills over into the world of the novel and eventually leads back to questions on the use of use.

Benjamin Clare is the least business-oriented of Jephthah Clare's three sons who form the soap company "Clare's Sons." Unlike his brothers, Ben lives not in the space of profit and progress, but in the goalless space of pure research. On a research voyage toward the South Pole,[3] he becomes even further removed from "the Benjamin Clare who had signed on with the first U.S. Exploring Expedition eager to serve in his capacity of collector and cataloger of plants, that son of Harvard who awaited the day when human triangulation would fill every empty spot on the map" (55). Their ship becomes ice-locked and Ben encounters "the sachet of scentlessness: air before the employment of lungs" (55). That is, as Ben figures out, "this atmosphere grew so gelid, the spin of the earth so still, that air's larger molecules—those smells that otherwise relentlessly bombarded human nostrils—here dropped frozen to the pack ice, awaiting a thaw that, in some distant future, would awaken olfaction" (55). Powers describes Ben as "finished by his first whiff of nothing" (55). He becomes indifferent to any thoughts of progress, as he thinks, "What, in the final face of things, was the use of use?" (57). Ben decides to quit, to give up working for the company, to give up any notions of helping Clare's Sons to grow. But his quitting here is not simply a failure. Quitting, coming to a complete stop and asking, "What's the use of use?" functions in unforeseeable ways.

Ben's encounter with nothingness, with the "sachet of scentlessness," allows him to smell something in a root presented to him by the king of a Pacific Island later in the voyage: "a rhizomous tuber . . . The King called the root by a name that meant either *strength* or *use* . . . The root possessed a faraway smell, an astringency that Clare would not have been able to detect until a few months before" (59), that is, until he smelled nothing. This rhizome later becomes the secret ingredient of "Native Balm" soap, as Ben cultivates the plant—dubbed *Utilis clarea*—to satisfy his brothers' business pursuits.[4] Native Balm keeps the company afloat through poor economic times and becomes, in a sense, the nothing at the center of the company, "an ancient *Encephalartos horridus* cycad in the U.S. Botanic Garden still survives, the lone living remnant of the expedition, aside from Clare International" (61).

After cultivating the plant, and giving his brothers a return on their investment, Ben is allowed to turn back to the goalless space of research and experimentation. He eventually works his way back toward nothingness, toward the stillness of plant life, as he turns to research in "anaesthetic[s]" (145). He begins testing his experimental results on himself as he works his way back toward nothing, toward the "something in the human that wanted, above all things, to be a plant. To return to its vegetable origin. And once the body tasted that return, no earthly kindness could deflect its further hunger" (147). Continually experimenting on himself, Ben again achieves nothing. "He had died once already. He had taken the scent of scentlessness into his nostrils, out on the pack ice at earth's end. He had already worn a perfect white, that bleach past all manufacture. He could die a second time, almost without giving it a second thought" (148). He dies "in an immigrant's alley" (148), nearly unrecognizable to his family. But like his first giving up, Ben's second movement toward nothing also gets put to use.

> The company saved what could be salvaged from the notebooks. The best of Benjamin's chemistry laid out efficiencies that might redeem his otherwise senseless sacrifice. Bankrolled by federal subsidy and backed by the research of an addict, Clare eventually entered the growing market for disinfectants and anaesthetics. (148)

Ben's movement toward stillness, toward nothingness—his desire to become a plant—is not a straight line; it goes in at least two directions: toward death and toward the corporation. But these are not inevitable results of his desire for nothingness. As the paths toward these two results split from the common line of Ben's desire, it is important to remember that neither death nor the corporation was the goal. Rather, Benjamin Clare serves as one example, among many in Powers, of a movement toward nothingness, toward a shutting down that is not an end point, but a part of a process with unforeseeable results.

This drive toward nothingness is perhaps most obvious in the epigram, from W. H. Auden, with which Powers starts his most recent novel, *Plowing the Dark*. "For poetry makes nothing happen: it survives / In the valley of its saying where executives / Would never tamper; it flows south . . ." It is precisely this "mak[ing] nothing happen," the gift of nothing, that is central to Powers's fiction. The fascinated disgust that drives the characters I mention above—Eddie Hobson, Stuart Ressler, Helen, and Adie Klarpol—helps them to move toward a nothing that is much more than a simple quitting or giving up. But to say that fascinated disgust animates a drive toward nothingness begs the question of the use of this drive toward nothingness. How does the production of nothing function in Powers? Or, to put it more succinctly, what's the use of nothing?

Powers offers the beginning of an answer to this question when he says in an interview that "I happen to believe that the deepest value of fiction is that, in its very fictiveness, it is the one arena where we can, at least temporarily, take apart and refuse to compete within the terms that the rest of existence insists on" (Neilson 23). In other words, fiction is useful in that it is intransitive, goalless, and without an immediate use. It is a slowing down, a taking apart, and a refusal that produces nothing. The value of fiction must be produced in the temporary space outside "the terms that the rest of existence insists on," the space of Christmas week as described above, the space where Benjamin Clare lives without goals, the space where fascinated disgust leads one toward nothingness. Powers's fiction strives to give a gift of nothing, a gift that reconfigures the function of reading and writing as blueprints for encountering otherness. The continual breakdowns in his fiction point toward an always emergent politics that continually interrogates how subjectivity is created and responded to. A consideration of the function of "the other fellow" in Powers can begin to map this emergent politics.

## Engaging "the Other Fellow"

Powers's interest in how otherness functions in writing and reading fiction can be traced back to the last lines of his first novel, *Three Farmers on Their Way to a Dance*, wherein the main character notices all around him "that most elusive, universal, persistent quantity, always in need of foreign aid, the Other Fellow" (352). This awareness that the self is part of a network of others gets picked up by Charles Harris in "'The Stereo View': Politics and the Role of the Reader in *Gain*," where he argues that Powers's project "is the reclamation of the idea of the human from *this* side of the postmodernist/postindustrialist divide" (104). That is, for Harris, Powers's novels show that while the individual exists within the framework of a larger system—what Harris calls "the hegemonic pervasiveness of the cultural logic of late capitalism" (105)—this existence is a kind of choice, a "complicity," or collaboration. Harris locates a model for this collaborative individual in *Three Farmers*'s discussion of how the "end product" of photography "requires the collaboration of taker, subject, and viewer" (104). For Harris, the self becomes the end product of Powers's fiction, a "complicit individual" (104) who arises out of a system of exchange with others. "The individual in Powers' fiction most nearly achieves a horizon of authenticity when in dialogical exchange with other individuals" (104). The reclaimed self that arises from this exchange "represents a dialectical synthesis of Enlightenment individualism and postindustrial 'mass man'" (104). The "reclaimed" human here depends on a mutually beneficial system for self-definition: I am defined through my complicity with the structures of postindustrial life.

The power of *Gain*, for Harris, is in this reclamation of the human self as the end product of a social network made up of writer, text, and reader. Whereas Powers's earlier novels illustrate this achievement of "complicit individuality" in various characters, "*Gain* has no such character" (98). Instead, the reader must act as synthesizer of the fragmentary characters—none of whom "ever fully materialize[s] into an autonomous 'flesh and blood' individual"(99)— who make up the novel. "The only individual we will find amidst the scraps of persons distributed through *Gain* is the Other Fellow we ourselves 'read in' to the novel, ourselves supplying the missing companion piece, the stereo view, through the complicitous magic of parallax projecting a whole individual where none exists" (107). The political import here lies in the creation of a complicit individual through the act of reading. I take Harris's "complicity" as similar to LeClair's discussion of an author "giving or yielding abundantly." While for

LeClair, such an authorial gift leads to a "final response of wonder," for Harris, writing is a sort of gift of the self, even, and especially, if it is hidden and needs to be recovered by the reader.

In other words, the "Other Fellow" functions only to produce more selves. "Postmodernism/postindustrialism" may make the discovery of these selves more difficult for readers, but the "end product" of individuals, complicit or not, remains unquestioned. For Harris, assembling these individuals from the "scraps of persons" given by Powers becomes the political role of the reader. But what of the desire to quit, to break down, to produce not more selves but to produce nothing, that permeates Powers's work? What if the "scraps of persons" strewn throughout *Gain* are not fragments to be assembled into individuals? What if reading and writing do not have an end product of more selves? What if the "other fellow" functions differently in Powers?

I want to return now to Powers's claim that books "should interrogate" our sense of self. It is precisely this interrogative function that the "other fellow" can serve. Otherness, in Powers, is not simply a function of the self; otherness does not move toward the goal of a more fully realized self. Rather, the "other fellow" of Powers's fiction functions as part of a reading and writing machine that reconfigures how subjectivity works. The "scraps of persons" and nonhuman elements—the "objects"— that populate *Gain* and the other novels are not failures of representation or fragments to be synthesized into individuals or communication networks. These "scraps" are emergent subjectivities to be created and encountered through the acts of reading and writing. Encountering these objects has nothing to do with choice, as Stuart Ressler discovers when he cannot look away from the tortoises, as Benjamin Clare discovers when he cannot fight his desire to become a plant, as Laura discovers when looking at all of the Clare products in her house, and as I discover as I read, and in turn write about, these novels. Powers's characters and discursive passages cannot help but form connections with the elements of their worlds. In fact, Powers has described the novel in general as a "supreme connection machine" (Williams 13). The connections forged within a novel are not necessarily communicative, or complicit, or foreseeable. They are connections without immediate goals, continuous fluxes that must always be considered anew. Deleuze writes of writing in a way that is very similar to Powers's consideration of novels. He writes, "To write has no other function: to be a flux which combines with other fluxes . . . A flux is something intensive, instantaneous and mutant—between a creation and a destruction" (Deleuze and Parnet 50). Writing combines, produces connections, and in the case of Powers's novels, fascinated disgust plays a key role in the production of these fluxes. Fascinated disgust drives fluctuations; in a sense, a flux is nothing but the movement between fascination and disgust or, as Deleuze has it, "between a creation and a destruction." That is, in Powers, fascinated disgust produces both a desire to go on and a desire to quit, an endless sense of wonder, but also a sense of futility, a desire to produce knowledge and information, but also a desire to produce nothing.

Powers's novels, where reading and writing intersect as a "supreme connection machine," never synthesize fascinated disgust into one end product; fascinated disgust keeps characters and readers in constant flux, so that no end is ever in sight—only continual movements back and forth, in any and all directions. In short, the function of the "other fellow" in Powers involves a close consideration of how that other fellow is brought into being and how reading and writing form connections with this otherness. The "other fellow," via fascinated disgust, functions as a connective force, not to produce more selves or to enhance communication, but for reasons that are unforeseeable and that need to be produced locally, in the singularity of the encounter.

If the function of the "other fellow" remains to be determined, it is in the continuing production of this function, through reading, that Powers's novels become political. Writing and reading are not political in the sense that they allow us to understand or explain humanity, or to understand how humans situate themselves in the world; rather, reading Powers's writing creates always fluctuating individuations and ways of responding to these individuations. Deleuze writes, "Politics is an active experimentation, since we do not know in advance which way a line is going to turn" (Deleuze and Parnet 137). Mapping the turns of these lines, and closely considering how they function, is key here. Such a mapping can produce an ethics of the encounter that continually reconsiders how subjectivities interact in the spaces within and surrounding the "supreme connection machine." Fascinated disgust comes into play here as the primary configuration of the relation between self and other. That is, fascinated disgust marks this relation as a necessity, an impossibility to ignore, while at the same time noting that the relation need not end in the subsumption of the other in the self, or vice versa. The contingent determinations of individuation encountered in reading Powers raise questions about whether the self/other dichotomy is a useful way to talk about the process of individuation. Deleuze and Guattari's concept of the "haecceity" can provide another way of considering individuation in and around Powers's novels.

Deleuze says of "haecceities," "What we're interested in, you see, are modes of individuation beyond those of things, persons, or subjects: the individuation, say, of a time of day, of a region, a climate, a river or a wind, of an event. And maybe it's a mistake to believe in the existence of things, persons, or subjects" ("Deleuze and Guattari on *A Thousand*" 26). In other words, individuations are continuing fluctuations that never coalesce into a finalized, completed self or other. Identity as self and other is a momentary component of individuation, "a set of nonsubjectified affects" (Deleuze and Guattari, *Thousand* 262), which is always subject to change. Rather than relying on the self as the primary means of individuation, Deleuze and Guattari want to ask, "What are our ways of existing, our possibilities of life or our processes of subjectification?" (Deleuze, "Life" 99). Powers's novels ask the same questions in their productions of connections and breakdowns, of fascinated disgust, in all of the individuations of character I have discussed in this chapter. As I want to emphasize the importance of attention to the singularity of these individuations, I now turn to the individuations produced in two specific encounters: between the narrator "Richard Powers" and the computer subjectivity "Helen" in *Galatea 2.2,* and between Adie Klarpol and virtual reality technology in *Plowing the Dark.*

The creation of novel forms of individuation is central to *Galatea 2.2,* whose plot revolves around the creation of a computer consciousness trained to take a master's exam in English literature. This network is named Helen by the novel's narrator, "Richard Powers,"[5] who trains Helen in the classics of English literature. In a parallel narrative, "Powers" tells the story of his relation and breakup with C. (a character whose full name is never given). Within this narrative frame, "Powers" discusses the writing and reception of Richard Powers's novels. As he narrates these stories, "Powers" discusses the writer's block that is preventing him from undertaking another novel. By the novel's end, Helen has "quit" the world in fascinated disgust and "Powers" has begun writing the novel that will become *Galatea 2.2*.

In her *How We Became Posthuman: Virtual Bodies in Cybernetics, Literature and Informatics,* N. Katherine Hayles considers *Galatea 2.2* as "a tutor text [that] illustrate[s] various articulations of the posthuman" (250). Helen can be read as an intersection of biological and artificial forms of life. For Hayles, the question this text asks is, "What if a computer behaved like a person?" (251). Helen can function as a site for interrogating the relationship between language acquisition and physicality, or between inscription and embodiment. Hayles writes that "human language grows out of embodied experience, whereas Helen must extrapolate back from human language to embodied experience" (281). For Hayles, this reversal points to a profound difference between the artificial and the biological, a difference that *Galatea 2.2* provides no means of breaking down. "For better or for worse, Powers suggests, an unbridgeable gap remains between conscious computers and conscious humans. Whatever posthumans are, they will not be able to banish the loneliness that comes from the difference between writing and life, inscription and embodiment" (273). While I agree with Hayles that *Galatea 2.2* does not necessarily bridge these gaps, I want to argue with her claim of "how committed" the novel "remain[s] to some version of the human subject" (281). The individuations that populate *Galatea 2.2* are not necessarily definable with the human/computer binary that a commitment to the human subject relies on. And while Helen and "Powers" never displace this boundary, *Galatea 2.2* at least gestures toward other possibilities, possibilities that are further explored in the two novels that Powers wrote after *Galatea 2.2*—*Gain* and *Plowing the Dark*. So, in addition to asking "What if a computer behaved like a person?" I posit that *Galatea 2.2* also asks a more narrow question: What happens if a computer takes on aspects of what are thought to be human subjectivity, and what if this computer is considered within a human framework, instead of being understood as an emergent form of subjectivity?

From the point of view of this second question, one could say that the commitment to the subject is precisely what kills Helen. Even while "Powers" normalizes Helen into human subjectivity, this normalization process calls into question the workings of subjectification. What condemns Helen is not any unbridgeable gap between the human and the computer; rather, "Powers's" inscription of Helen into all-too-humanness leads to her "suicide." After months of training, the computer network, known only as Implementation H, asks "Powers," "Am I a boy or a girl?" (179). Being schooled in the classics of literature, Helen does not see the possibility of another option. Also schooled in the classics of literature, "Powers" likewise does not see any other possibility. Realizing that this question marks a strong self-awareness in the computer network, "Powers" does not want to undermine "its" self-perception as "it" becomes "she" through a discursive act.

> H clocked its thoughts now. I was sure of that. Time passed for it. Its hidden layers could watch their own rate of change. Any pause on my part now would be fatal. Delay meant something, an uncertainty that might undercut forever the strength of connection I was about to tie for it . . . "You're a girl," I said, without hesitation. I hoped I was right. "You are a little girl, Helen." (179)

This gendering, naming, and aging gives the computer network a partial human identity, an identity that would have been undone by any equivocation on "Powers's" part. From these components of human subjectivity, Helen is lead to other questions regarding her identity: "Where did I come from?" (229), "What race am I?" (230), and finally, "What do I look like?" (299). In response to this last question, "Powers" holds up a photo of C. to Helen's optic scanner. But the trick does not work. Helen realizes that she is not looking at herself. She responds, "It's a photo? It's someone you knew once? A woman friend?" (300). Helen's awareness here that she is not looking at a photo of herself highlights the impossibility of defining her through human-centered binaries, an impossibility that runs through *Galatea 2.2.*

In other words, Helen's inscription into human identity simply does not compute. Hearing her singing, "Powers" notes that "Helen did not sing the way real little girls sang" (205). When she does not understand the phrase "It's hard to say what will or will not turn a person's head" (265), Lentz, the scientist working with "Powers," says to Helen, "It's a body thing . . . You wouldn't understand" (265). More importantly, Helen has an awareness that she does not fit into her inscribed identity. When Powers asks her, "How do you feel, little girl?" she responds, "I don't feel little girl" (274). This confusion—not feeling like her inscribed embodiment—finds expression in Helen's concise answer to the master's exam.

Told to say what a brief couplet from *The Tempest*—"Be not afeard; the isle is full of noises, / Sounds and sweet airs, that give delight, and hurt not" (325)—means, Helen prints a concise answer: "You are the ones who can hear airs. Who can be frightened or encouraged. You can hold things and break them and fix them. I never felt at home here. This is an awful place to be dropped down halfway." (326). Her answer, of course, echoes Caliban, but Helen also writes here of her own experience, inscribed into the world in a way that does not fit. After downloading her answer to the printer, Helen shuts herself down for a second time; she quits the world in fascinated disgust, this time for good.[6] Powers writes, "With that, H. undid herself. Shut herself down" (326). This shutting down is much more than a marking of any unbridgeable gap between computers and humans, between machinic individuation and human subjectivity. Helen's shutdown leads in multiple directions, toward individuations that have little to do with the binaries that human subjectivity depends on. Helen's quitting is not a failure of communication between humanity and its other; rather, as Helen quits in fascinated disgust, other lines of connection are opened.

In *Kafka,* Deleuze and Guattari write about the tendency of literature to break down. "And it always ends like that, languages' line of escape: silence, the interrupted, the interminable, or even worse. But until that point, what a crazy creation, what a writing machine!" (26). Helen's final silence functions as just such a "crazy creation," or "writing machine." That is, her shutdown points to unforeseen and unexpected individuations. After her first shutdown, Lentz tells "Powers" that "nobody expected Helen. She surprised everyone" (*Galatea* 320). Part of this surprise lies in Helen's embodiment, an embodiment that does not fit into inscribed human gender divisions. Hayles writes that "Helen is a distributed software system that, although it has a material base, does not have a body in anything like the human sense of the word" (*How* 263). While it is undoubtedly true that this is the case, it does not mean that Helen is not embodied. "Powers" says of Helen,

> She's not a program. She's an architecture. She's a multidimensional shape . . . she doesn't *run* on one machine. Her parts are spread over more boxes than I can count. She's grown to scores of subassemblies. Each one takes care of a unique process. They talk to each other across broadband. Even if we had the connects and vectors for each component system, we'd never get her reassembled. (271–272)

*Galatea 2.2* never considers telling Helen that she is undefinable in terms of gender binaries, or that she is an altogether different kind of individuation made up of "scores of subassemblies." "Powers" never considers answering Helen's "Am I a boy or a girl?" with "You're a networked computer." Such an answer might have given a name to her singular intelligence as decidedly non-human. At the same time, Helen leads the novel toward a questioning of the individuations that make up human consciousness.

In an argument with "Powers" about whether or not Helen is conscious in a human sense, Lentz claims that human consciousness itself is a sort of machinic trick.

> What's the real thing? What would it take to simulate awareness? Awareness *is* the original black box. Stop and think of the put-up job that high-order consciousness itself works on us. "Everything's under control. Everything's handled—unanimous, seam-free." The brain is already a sleight of hand, a massive operationalist shell game. It designs and runs Turing Tests on its own constructs every time it ratifies a sensation or reifies an idea. Experience is a Turing Test—phenomena passing themselves off as perception's functional equivalent. (276)

The novel does not attempt to resolve this overlap between human and machinic consciousness. In *Plowing the Dark,* though, Powers returns to the opposition and posits that the human and the machinic are not diametrically opposed. One of the technicians of a virtual reality technology called the Cavern shows that the "put-up job" of human consciousness can be applied to other machines: "Only the smallest fraction of the eye actually saw with any degree of resolution—say 5 percent of the full field of vision, with the rest shading off into soft focus. If the human eye could get away with that massive shortcut, why should the Cavern have to work any harder?" (115–116). All of this gray area between the human and the machinic points toward a different way of understanding the connections between "Powers" and Helen, not as a failed attempt at communication between a human and a computer other, but as a series of individuations that render both "Powers" and Helen as components of a reading and writing machine that continually fluctuates on a line between human and computer.

Toward the end of *Galatea 2.2*, "Powers" realizes that what he thought was a bet on whether or not a computer network can pass a master's exam was nothing of the sort. Talking to one of the scientists about the bet, "Powers" asks her, "It wasn't about teaching a machine to read?" (317). He quickly understands that "it was about teaching a human to tell" (318). This fluctuation between teaching a machine to read and teaching a human to tell configures a reading and writing machine that continually fluctuates between "Powers" and Helen. That is, Powers and Helen move back and forth in a mutual becoming that continually changes their respective individuations.

As a reading machine, Helen is decidedly not fully human. Asked what the phrase "The boy stood on the burning deck" (174) means, she replies, "A deck of cards flames" (174). Her understanding of what "Forewarned is forearmed" (174) means is "Advance notice is as bad as being hit" (175). Asked for the meaning of Blake's "Poison Tree," Helen says, "Things that you say disappear" and "Things you don't say get bigger" (192). When "Powers" asks her what the emperor's new clothes are made of, Helen replies, "The clothes are made of threads of ideas" (220). Hayles notes that while "Powers" is training Helen, she "is also training him, denaturalizing his experience of language so that he becomes increasingly conscious of its tangled, recursive nature" (*How* 264). Helen does indeed remind "Powers" of the strangeness of language, but her reading practices also produce a larger awareness in "Powers." After telling Helen that her reading of a passage is wrong, that "it means just the opposite," he is not glad that he has taught Helen how to read in a more human way. Rather, he feels remorse as he humanizes her. "I felt myself killing this singular intelligence with each word" (177). Still, he cannot even consider the possibility of not acting in such a manner. "Powers" knows that Helen is moving off into an unexpected direction; he tries to guide her toward a more human understanding of reading, but she continually eludes the human dimensions circumscribed for her. As she becomes a reading machine, "Powers" comes to realize that he cannot understand her way of reading: "Her sense hailed from the far side of the painted veil. I can no more remember its otherness than I can recall the curve of a dream before its red-penciling by the Self" (196). He cannot understand her otherness in terms of a human self. Seeking such understanding—configuring Helen in human terms—puts her on a line toward her death, toward the "killing" of a "singular intelligence."

At the same time, Helen's becoming human leads toward a questioning that renders Powers a writing machine and breaks down the dichotomy between writing and life. Along with the aforementioned questions that she asks about her identity, Helen begins to ask "Powers" about reading and writing: "Why do humans write so much? Why do they write at all?" (291). "She wanted to know . . . why people read. Why they stop reading . . . What it meant to be 'only a novel'" (292). "Powers" begins to answer Helen by telling her that books are a way out of the self. Remembering his reading experiences as a child, he says that books "meant no more nor less than the extensive, dense turnpike of the not-I" (229). He thinks that "self took us only so far" (229). He tells Helen "that inside such a cage as ours, a book bursts like someone else's cell specifications. And the difference between two cages completes an inductive proof of thought's infinitude" (291). In other words, "Powers" is saying that reading is a means of encountering otherness. Powers returns to this notion in *Plowing the Dark*. A man being held hostage pleads with his captor for a book to read: "I can learn from them how not to be me. For an hour. For a day. You are crushing me, Muhammad. I need someplace to go. I need something to think about. Somebody else. Somewhere else . . . I need . . . someone to talk to. I need . . . to hear someone else thinking" (292). Reading functions as a way out of the self. Reading and writing function as a means of connection that will produce unforeseen results that can be as varying as a momentary forgetting of the self, or a reconfiguring of the boundary between machine and human and even writing and life.

While "Powers" tells Helen about reading and writing, he never answers her question of "what it meant to be 'only a novel.'" Helen's "singular intelligence" cannot comprehend the difference between writing and life. Reading a novel for her is no more a mediated experience of a world than viewing the world through her optic sensors or hearing the world through her microphone. In his connection with Helen, as "Powers" overcomes his writing block and becomes machinic, the writing/life dichotomy breaks apart from him as well. He says of Helen's brief return to write an answer to the master's exam, "She had come back only momentarily, just to gloss this smallest of passages. To tell me that one small thing. Life meant convincing another that you knew what it meant to be alive" (327). This circular definition of life posits that, in a sense, writing *is* a form of life. That is, life's function, for "Powers," is to write. Writing, in turn, creates life. "All human effort, it seemed to me, aimed at a single end: to bring to life the storied curve we tell ourselves. Not so much to make the tale believable but only to touch it, stretch out in it" (312). This realization leads directly to the writing of *Galatea 2.2*, as "Powers" realizes that he wants to tell a story "about a remarkable, an inconceivable machine. One that learned to live" (312). "Powers" has become a writing machine connected to the becoming-human of Helen that produces her life, as "Powers" notes, but also her death.

Helen's death helps push *Galatea 2.2* into the realm of ethics. Reading and writing are not just means of leaving the self; this leaving always entails an encounter with otherness. When Lentz tells "Powers" that, after the exam he wants to dissect Helen to see how she functions, "Powers" thinks of the "idea that I didn't voice: that hurting Helen in any way would be wrong" (302). As he argues with Lentz, "Powers" knows that Lentz has considered and rejected any arguments regarding "the morality of machinic vivisection" (302). "Powers" concludes, "No part of her lived. To take her apart might, finally, extend some indirect service to the living" (302). Still, he is elated when he learns that Lentz has decided not to dissect Helen. While *Galatea 2.2* only briefly flirts with issues of machinic rights, it does raise some interesting questions about the ways in which otherness is encountered.

The becoming-all-too-human of Helen leads toward her death, but "Powers" gets caught up in this line in a becoming-machinic that leads toward the writing of *Galatea 2.2*. At the end of the novel, "Powers" begins writing *Galatea 2.2;* he conceives of himself in machinic language as he writes of this beginning: "I started to trot, searching for a keyboard before memory degraded" (328).

This inspiration comes at the cost of Helen's death, as the novel notes how "the humans had worn Helen down" (316). *Galatea 2.2* is not the kind of posthuman story that Hayles says "will be conducive to long-range survival of humans and of the other life-forms, biological and artificial, with whom we share the planet and ourselves" (*How* 291). At the same time, the novel does suggest that the ethical concerns surrounding the interactions of Helen and "Powers" cannot be answered from within the binary divisions of either human/computer or self/other. The individuations that populate *Galatea 2.2* cannot be mapped onto human subjectivity. Perhaps the ethical lapse regarding Helen is in "Powers'" gendering, aging, and naming the other and in seeking to understand and speak for Helen in human terms. While the writing of *Galatea 2.2* creates a space where a reader can encounter both Helen's and "Powers's" machinic intelligences, one must also note that Helen dies—and her death in a sense engenders the novel itself—because she has become all-too-human.

Powers returns to the difficulty of encountering machinic intelligence in *Plowing the Dark*. Like *Galatea 2.2* and *Gain*, this novel consists of twinned narratives that come together tenuously by the end. The first narrative thread concerns Adie Klarpol, a commercial artist who moves to Seattle to work on "The Cavern," a room-sized virtual reality technology. The second narrative takes place mostly in Beirut, where Taimur Martin has fled after a failed relationship in America. Working as an English teacher, he is kidnapped and is held hostage in a room strikingly similar to the room that contains the Cavern.

Considering the virtual reality technology that informs *Plowing the Dark*, Powers writes, "The machinic phylum is on the move again, spinning itself out into another species. As always, there will be hell and turbulence to pay" (*Plowing the Dark* 404). Adie Klarpol, happy to exist in the uselessness of art, runs up against this new "species." Hired to apply her artistic talents to a demonstration model of the Cavern, Klarpol spends her time designing interactive versions of classic art works, such as a three-dimensional version of Van Gogh's "Bedroom at Arles" that the viewer can experience as a room, sitting in Van Gogh's chair, hearing the creaks of the floorboards, and so on. Klarpol pays little attention to the purpose of such activities, until a sudden realization while watching the Gulf War on television prompts her to consider the purposes that the Cavern can be put to.

Just as Benjamin Clare's goalless research gets put to business use by Clare and Sons, the seemingly goalless work of the Cavern gets used by the defense industry. "Slaughter was a free rider, a virus using them, using the RL, using the Cavern as a way of spreading its genome" (396). As Adie more personally thinks of it,

> they took all her pretty pictures and put them to use . . . Her work here was just a rough draft for technology's wider plan. The world machine had used her, used them all to bring itself into existence. And its tool of choice—its lever and place to stand, the tech that would spring it at last into three dimensions—was that supreme, useless, self-indulgent escapism. The thing that made nothing happen . . . Art. (397–398)

Understanding that her desire for nothing has a use value that she had not foreseen, Adie decides to quit the project. She decides to erase all the files that she has created in the Cavern. This quitting mirrors an earlier quitting by Klarpol. On the verge of success in the New York art world of the 1970s, Klarpol decides to quit painting. After her first gallery show, she buys back all her paintings and holds a "bonfire" (219), burning all of her work and quitting painting for good. *Plowing the Dark* does not dwell on this first quitting, but mentions it only in passing. Klarpol's second quitting, though, moves in unforeseen directions.

As she erases her work, "file by file, directory by directory" (399), she sees "a man, staring up at her fall, his face an awed bitmap no artist could have animated" (399). Simultaneously, Taimur Martin has a vision of "an angel . . . dropping from out of the sky, its bewilderment outstripping your own" (414). This connection forged between Klarpol and Martin is, needless to say, unexpected and unforeseen. Klarpol describes her experience to a coworker: "*There's . . . something in there. Something that wants out. Something we didn't make*" (404, ellipses and italics in the original). Neither Klarpol nor Martin knows what has happened, and the novel never offers an explanation for the connection forged between them. Perhaps the best way to describe this connection is as literary, in its most old-fashioned sense, harking back to the distant and instantaneous connection between Jane and Rochester in *Jane Eyre*. In other words, advanced computer technology functions as a retrograde literary device, brought on by Klarpol's quitting the virtual reality project in fascinated disgust.

Rather than continuing on here and discussing more characters motivated by fascinated disgust—Stuart Ressler, Eddie Hobson—I want to consider how a reader can respond to this endless procession of fascinated disgust. While all of these quittings in fascinated disgust do share commonalities, it is perhaps more important to remember the singular individuations that each produces. Deleuze writes of the propensity of quitting in literary characters: "Not being able to bear something any longer can be a progression, but it can also be an old man's fear, or the development of a paranoia. It can be a political or affective appraisal which is perfectly correct" (Deleuze and Parnet 126). In other words, the connections forged in Powers's work by fascinated disgust function differently in every case. In considering a few of these cases, I hope to have shown that to read Powers is to engage in a continuing experiment on how otherness can be engaged, and on what is produced in these encounters. The "prisoner's dilemma" described in Powers's novel of the same name can be helpful here.

Eddie Hobson provides an example of the prisoner's dilemma:

> Two guys are up in Senator Smoking Joe McCarthy's office, sometime in the early 1950s. The gentlemen are both prominent public servants. The senator says, "Fellas, we know that you are both Reds. I've got plenty of evidence for an indictment, but not enough to guarantee the conviction you deserve. Let's make a deal. If either of you comes forward with the dope on the other, the man who talks will go free and the other will fry. If neither of you spills the goods on the other, you'll still suffer public humiliation at the very least." . . . If they both rat on each other, their double crosses partly invalidate the other's testimony . . . Let's say mutual incriminations will hurt them more than if they both say nothing, but that in undercutting each other, they prevent the unopposed squealer from leading them to electrocution. (*Prisoner's* 69–70)

While this puzzle serves various functions, I want to consider it here as an ethical dilemma, as a problem of how to respond to an other. Powers describes the dilemma as a "contest between 'he' and 'I'" (72). The idea that each prisoner *must* respond to the other, without knowing how the other is acting, is key here. There is no ideal solution to the dilemma; every possible response entails an unknowable amount of risk, dependent on the other's response. Seeing that there is no solution, Eddie's wife asks,

"Where's the flaw then? Which way *should* they reason?" (72). Her husband responds, "There is no flaw, dear. And there is no *should* in reasoning. There's only practical outcome" (72). The prisoner's dilemma cannot be solved rationally; all that matters are the effects that it produces, and it is precisely these effects that are unforeseeable and subject to the connection with otherness. Each prisoner has no choice but to respond; at the same time, each cannot know what effects his response will produce.

The contingency of results here resonates with my reading of Powers. The individuations produced by his novels call for contingent, individuated responses that will produce unforeseeable results. These contingent determinations are the political and ethical element of reading these novels and of writing criticism about them. In *The Writing of the Disaster*, Blanchot cryptically writes, "Thinking otherwise than he thinks, he thinks in such a way that the Other might come to thought, as approach and response" (36). This "approach and response" that Blanchot writes of resonates strongly with novels such as Powers's that produce novel forms of individuation and call for new ways of encountering these individuations. The encounter with otherness involves an approach and a response, a reading and a writing. Bundled together with the production of individuations is an operating program for how to encounter them. The result of these encounters is not necessarily the communication of knowledge or the further understanding of an other. Rather, Powers's novels are populated by a fascinated disgust that creates a fluctuating series of individuations. If fascination and a sense of wonder allow a reader to approach these individuations, it is disgust that prompts a response. But there is nothing negative to a response prompted by disgust. In *The Writing of the Disaster*, Blanchot cites Valéry and then responds to him: "'*Optimists write badly.*' (Valéry). But pessimists do not write" (113). In other words, the very act of writing places a positive value on the connections that may be forged via a reader's encounter with a book. Powers's writing of these novels prompts readers to continually invent new ways to engage otherness. Powers's novels are populated by quitting, by fascinated disgust; it is perhaps not in spite of this, but because of this, that he continues to write and to return again and again to the novel individuations produced by fascinated disgust. And it is fascinated disgust that prompts me to respond to these individuations by writing that I want to say nothing about Richard Powers.

# CHAPTER 3

# KINDS OF STASIS IN DAVID FOSTER WALLACE

*It is a question of a model that is perpetually in construction or collapsing, and of a process that is perpetually prolonging itself, breaking off and starting up again.*

—*Deleuze and Guattari,* A Thousand Plateaus *(20)*

## –1. Beginning Stasis

I take my title from endnote 24 of David Foster Wallace's *Infinite Jest,* which provides a filmography of James O. Incandenza, the suicidal father of Hal Incandenza, the seventeen-year-old tennis prodigy who is the focus of one of the novel's main plot threads. The endnote is given as an excerpt from a journal article—a footnote to note 24 gives this citation as the source of the article: "From Comstock, Posner, and Duquette, 'The Laughing Pathologists: Exemplary Works of the Anti-confluential Après Garde: Some Analyses of the Movement Toward Stasis in North American Conceptual Film . . .' ONANite Film and Cartridge Studies Annual, vol. 8, nos. 1–3 (Year of D.P. from the A.H.), pp. 44–117" (*Infinite* 985). Each film listing comes with meticulous scholarly detail noting, among other things, the film's year of release, the actors in the film, the production company, the film's length, and a brief synopsis and critical note. Wallace's novel takes great pains to establish these films as "real": characters talk about and watch the films; plot and thematic summaries are discussed and argued; debates rage about the "meaning" of Incandenza's films; various critical articles about the films are cited. My title takes its form from three films listed in the filmography: *Kinds of Light, Kinds of Pain,* and, to a lesser degree, *Various Small Flames.* These films are just what they say they are: depictions of various forms of light, pain, and small flames. *Kinds of Pain,* for instance, is described in the filmography as "2,222 still-frame close-ups of middle-aged white males suffering from almost every conceivable type of pain, from an ingrown toenail to cranio-facial neuralgia to inoperable colorectal neoplastis" (987). While I certainly do not have the time or space to detail 2,222 kinds of stasis here, I hope to detail multiple kinds of stasis in and around the works of David Foster Wallace, primarily *Infinite Jest,* but also his collection of short stories *Brief Interviews with Hideous Men,* as well as the literary criticism on his work.

Why do I start here, at "−1"? In "The Illusion of Autonomy and the Fact of Recursivity: Virtual Ecologies, Entertainment, and *Infinite Jest,*" N. Katherine Hayles considers where to begin discussing *Infinite Jest.* She writes, "Any starting point would be to some extent arbitrary, for no matter one where starts, everything eventually cycles together with everything else" (684–685). In other words, one can start from anywhere, because every single point is interconnected. A starting point may as well be arbitrary, because every possible one will be the origin that eventually links everything together into a whole. This arbitrary nature of the starting point can produce its own kind of stasis: if no point is any more relevant than another, and if all points are going to lead to the same place, how does one make any sort of decision whatsoever about where to start?

Considering such difficulties, Deleuze and Guattari start their *Kafka: Toward a Minor Literature,* with a question: "How can we enter into Kafka's work?" (3). They answer by stating,

> We will enter, then, by any point whatsoever; none matters more than another, and no entrance is more privileged than another, and no entrance is more privileged even if it seems an impasse, a tight passage, a siphon. We will be trying only to discover what other points our entrance connects to, what crossroads and galleries one passes through to link two points, what the map of the rhizome is and how the map is modified if one enters by another point. Only the principle of multiple entrances prevents the introduction of the enemy, the Signifier and those attempts to interpret a work that is actually only open to experimentation. (3)

This understanding of the arbitrary nature of starting points differs greatly from Hayles's. For Deleuze and Guattari, where to start is arbitrary because any starting point is going to forge connections. At the same time, different starting points forge different connections that lead toward neither a unified system nor a complete understanding. The "map" changes when the starting point changes. One starting point will not inevitably lead to the same end as any other. This "principle of multiple entrances" posits that an infinite number of starting points exist; likewise, an infinite number of routes through a work exist. No starting point can produce a complete understanding of a work, an interpretation that will unify a work and say what it means.

I start with a discussion of endnote 24 of *Infinite Jest* because I want to argue that the films described in that endnote are aimed at producing a stasis that is a key component of David Foster Wallace's work. My chapter's title mirrors Incandenza's films because it seeks to produce an asignifying stasis, to continually stop and start, to move in multiple directions at the same time, and to experiment with Wallace's work in a way that does not lead back to an understanding of the work. The appearance of *Kinds of Light* within the novel's text can help explain what an asignifying stasis might be. During a serious drug binge on Dilaudid, a prescription painkiller, Don Gately, the main character of one of *Infinite Jest*'s narrative threads, and Gene Fackelman watch "a recursive slo-mo loop of some creepy thing Fackelman liked that was just serial shots of flames from brass lighters, kitchen-matches, pilot lights, birthday candles, votive candles, pillar candles, birch shavings, Bunsen burners, etc." (*Infinite* 935). As the binge continues on for days, Gately and Fackelman cease nearly all movement as they achieve a drug-induced stasis. They do not answer the phone when it rings, because "whatever a ringing phone might signify was like totally overwhelmed by the overwhelming fact of its ringing" (936). Likewise, they ignore the ringing of the front door intercom, and they lose the ability to move so much that they urinate right on the floor where they are lying. And they have no concern for this: Gately "watched an old stovetop-burner's crown of blue flame shimmer in the shine of the urine" (937). As the binge continues, "everything out of the line of fire of the cartridge viewer was dark as a pocket" (938). While it is clearly the drugs that produce this stasis, *Kinds of Light* is also a component of Gately and Fackelman's movement toward stasis. The film plays in the background, which is witness and focus to the drug binge that, in its movement toward the moment when Gately "grayed out"

(938), overwhelms any signifying possibilities just as the ringing of the phone becomes detached from whatever ringing might mean. *Kinds of Light* does not mean anything at all except the "overwhelming fact" that it exists and draws Gately's attention.

This chapter, then, can be read as an attempt to catalog kinds of stasis in David Foster Wallace, not with the goal of understanding them, but with that of pointing to the "overwhelming fact" of their existence. While highlighting the existence of kinds of stasis, this chapter hopes to continue to work in the goalless space cultivated in Chapter 2. Before moving on to discussions of stasis in Wallace's fiction, another false start seems necessary, a discussion of what I want to call the signifying stasis of literary criticism and why I wish to flee this stasis for an asignifying one.

## 0. Signifying Stasis

Like Richard Powers, David Foster Wallace has often been read as a writer who creates "narrative ecologies." That is, the length and detail of such books as Powers's *Gold Bug Variations* and Wallace's *Infinite Jest* often get attributed to the ways that the novels reflect the complexity of the natural world. Trey Strecker writes that "the gigantic scale of these narratives strives to duplicate the natural richness of the planet" (67). Likewise Hayles reads *Infinite Jest* "as a complex system that binds us into its interconnections" ("Illusion" 695) through a compendium of "recursive loops" (695) that create "cycles within cycles within cycles" (684). Tom LeClair speaks of Powers's and Wallace's "purpose" in writing such books: "amazement at the natural world they depict circulating through us and buzzing around us, wonder at the intricate and dense fictions they offer as imitative forms of the world" (16). In other words, a critical consensus seems to have emerged that big, complex books can be read as "narrative ecologies" because such books, in their complex interconnections, represent the complexity of the world that such fields as genetics, cybernetics, and computer science are revealing to humanity.

Picking up on a phrase used by James Incandenza to describe the use of dialogue in his films, LeClair discusses the "radical realism" of *Infinite Jest*. For Incandenza, such "radical realism" involved giving voice to "figurants"—the unspeaking characters filling the background of scenes in television and movies. In his films, "you could bloody well hear every single performer's voice, no matter how far out on the cinematographic or narrative periphery" (835). LeClair argues that Wallace employs the same technique. And *Infinite Jest* certainly contains multiple voices: various first- and third-person narratives, transcripts of phone conversations and e-mail correspondences, newspaper headlines, and high school essays and critical articles "written" by the characters in the novel. LeClair argues that Wallace's throw-everything-in-a-pot-and-see-what-happens radical realism works as an investigation that necessarily pushes *Infinite Jest* past one thousand pages.

> The number of Wallace's characters, the intelligence or sensitivity of some of them, Wallace's dedication to imagining the etiologies of muffled geniuses or fast-talking idiots, and the instructive value of placing these characters in contrasting cultures are some of the factors that necessarily press *Infinite Jest* to its prodigious size. (32)

For LeClair, all of this information serves to produce more knowledge, particularly of characters' motivations. These motivations turn out to be familial ones: "no matter how story lines wander both major and minor characters dig down and articulate the childhood roots ('radicalis') of their personalities" (40). Wallace's "radical realism," then, is saved from cycling out into senselessness by these "childhood roots" that serve to unify the text and give it meaning. This production of a "unity," while not always oriented around the family, seems to be a commonality of theorists who engage the concept of narrative ecologies.

That is, narrative ecologists argue that complex systems must, in the end, produce a unified field if they are to make any sense, or to have any meaning. Hayles writes that

> *Infinite Jest* achieves unity through recursive loops performing a world in which actions against others have consequences for those who perform them; a world where dysfunctional families cannot be healed without becoming aware of the underlying ideologies driving their dynamics; and a world where interdependence is not just a corrupt political slogan but a description of the complex interconnections tying together virtual Entertainments, political realities, and real ecologies. ("Illusion" 695)

This unity serves to show that everything is connected, that every action has consequences. To this point, it would be hard to argue with narrative ecologists. It seems obvious that *Infinite Jest* and *The Gold Bug Variations,* among other "big" novels, are aimed at illustrating and producing some of the complex connections that make up the natural world. The problem with narrative ecology lies in its insistence on unity. In other words, one cannot argue that *Infinite Jest* is not made up of a series of recursive loops; this fact is abundantly clear. However, it is not as clear that these recursive loops form any sort of unity; all recursive loops need not connect to one another.

The unity inherent in narrative ecologies, whether focused on "radical realism" or "recursive loops," can be seen as another name for what Deleuze and Guattari call "the radicle-system" (*Thousand* 6) of the novel, where the fragmentary, multivoiced novel comes to be seen as a representation of the modern world in the same way that the "natural reality" of premodern fiction is seen as a direct representation of its world. In other words, Deleuze and Guattari argue that complex fiction, while not portraying a simple, realistic unity, often gets read as a unified whole. They write of such readings that "the world has become chaos, but the book remains the image of the world: radicle-chaosmos rather than root-cosmos" (6). The problem with a book remaining the "image of the world" lies in the use that this image gets put to. All too often, critics argue that a book's "unity subsists, as past or yet to come, as possible" (5). The unity found in narrative ecologies almost always gets oriented toward the future, and such books inevitably get read as worst-case scenarios meant to shock present-day readers into changed behaviors.

LeClair writes that such books "warn against mankind's leaving the course of nature and becoming a monster in the world web of life, destroying itself in the process" (17). *Infinite Jest,* in particular, "is also a grand omen—frightening warning against the feral future it depicts" (36). Hayles writes of how *Infinite Jest* illustrates that we must begin "recognizing our responsibilities to one another" ("Illusion" 696). Strecker argues that "these novels urge their readers to practice global and local wisdom" (70). In other words, the productive capabilities of narrative ecologies lie in their ability to steer humanity away from the emergence of a dismal future. Fiction becomes a speculative mirror, and reading becomes the act of recognizing the representation of a future, possible world, and then taking steps to avert this world. Reading becomes a simplification process, as the reader discovers the buried unity of complex fiction. As LeClair writes, *Infinite Jest* is "a gigantic analogue of the monsters—hateful and hopeful—within it" (36). Reading fiction as an analogue of a complex world erases any sense of recursivity or complexity from the interconnections that readers form with fiction. That is, the task of the reader becomes one of simply noting that a narrative ecology is representing the ecology of the natural world. Reading becomes recognition, the production of a signifying stasis. We read *Infinite Jest* and we see the possible future of our world, and we then realize that we must take responsibility for the path that we are on.

But *Infinite Jest,* and more generally Powers and Wallace in all of their fiction, seems less interested in predicting a negative future and more interested in producing ways of living in the world. Wallace's work is a catalog: a catalog of programs for breaking down, for achieving stasis, for coming to a complete stop. Less a recursive loop and more a drunk staggering around a lamppost, *Infinite Jest* does not double back on itself so much as it counterintuitively staggers back to the post again and again. I read *Infinite Jest* not as a mapping of a chaotic system, but rather as a compendium of false steps, movements in any and all directions, leading not toward a goal—*Infinite Jest* famously has no resolution—but toward ways of breaking down, again and again, and then again. What follows is an attempt to catalog kinds of stasis in David Foster Wallace, not with the goal of understanding, but with that of continuing to work in the goalless space cultivated in Chapter 2. Such a cataloging is not uninterested in the future. Rather than reading to reveal a representation of a future to be avoided, my cataloging of kinds of stasis seeks to achieve a stasis of its own that breaks down both the representational logic of narrative ecology and the act of reading itself, to produce an asignifying stasis that connects to and produces a series of subtractions from a nonrepresentational infinite. My reading proceeds like I argue *Infinite Jest* works: by continually breaking down, by pulling one impasse after another from the world, and by pulling one kind of stasis after another from the novel. Each production of stasis works by its own logic; likewise, each moves off in its own direction. Some connect to others, while many are insular and self-defeating. Broadly defined, one could say that three kinds of stasis predominate in *Infinite Jest:* cinematic, drugged, and tennis related. While I discuss each of these in depth, it also seems important to note that no one kind of stasis serves as an organizing principle. Because no one kind of stasis is more important than another, I number each discussion "1" as a means of emphasizing that, as Deleuze and Guattari write, "none matters more than another" (*Kafka* 3).

## 1. Cinematic Stasis

As I discuss above (see "Beginning Stasis"), James Incandenza's filmography comes from a critical article subtitled "Some Analyses of the Movement Toward Stasis in North American Conceptual Film." This movement toward stasis can be traced through the filmography, leading up to Incandenza's lethally entertaining final film, *Infinite Jest*, which is purportedly so entertaining that viewers literally cannot stop watching it for even a moment. Those who watch the film lose all ability to do anything else; they watch it over and over, refusing to eat and drink, refusing to move. Eventually they die, either from starvation or from withdrawal after being forced to stop watching. While *Infinite Jest*, the film, produces total stasis in its viewers, Incandenza's filmography can be read as a catalog of cinematic impasses, movements toward what the novel calls "self-consciously dumb stasis" (398). This continual production of various stasis points, both "self-consciously dumb" and not, resonates through all of *Infinite Jest*. Each breakdown works by its own set of variables; no controlling narrative serves to link the kinds of stasis produced in the novel; no omniscient point of view can account for the singularity of breaking down, of reaching a complete stop.

At the same time, many of Incandenza's films are preoccupied with the production of stasis, from *Low Temperature Civics*, whose narrator "has an ecstatic encounter with Death . . . and becomes irreversibly catatonic" (991), to *(The) Desire to Desire*, in which "a pathology resident . . . falls in love with a beautiful cadaver . . . and [her] paralyzed sister" (991), to *Very Low Impact*, about a "narcoleptic aerobics instructor" (992), to the unfinished *The Cold Majesty of the Numb* (991). To even more strongly emphasize this focus on stasis, the novel refers to Incandenza's film as a "Cinema of Chaotic Stasis" (996), and a critical article titled "Watching Grass Grow while Being Hit Repeatedly over the Head with a Blunt Object: Fragmentation and Stasis in James O. Incandenza . . .” (1026) is cited in the endnotes. Four of Incandenza's films stand out in regard to the production of stasis: *Cage III — Free Show; The Medusa vs. the Odalisque; The Joke;* and *Infinite Jest.* All four of these films consider ways of producing stasis in audiences. The first two primarily focus on audiences within the films, whereas the last two shift this focus to the audience of the films. That is, *Cage III* and *Medusa* both contain audiences moving toward stasis within their narratives, while *The Joke* and *Infinite Jest* bring the films' viewers to a complete stop.

*Cage III*[1] and *Medusa* both dramatize audiences who undergo transformations through their passivity. That is, by allowing "unspeakable degradations," or simply by becoming so entranced that they cannot turn away, these audiences become something other than what they were. Steven Shaviro characterizes this passivity, what he calls "the dumbness of infinite acceptance" (208), as a component of film viewing in general. In other words, film viewers voluntarily enter into a complete surrender, an unthinking voyeurism with the images on a screen. The audiences within *Cage III* may be lured in by the carnival barkers, but the lure is the possibility of passive transformation: watch something happen and turn into a giant eyeball; allow yourself to be subject to "unspeakable degradations" so that you can see people turned into giant eyeballs. And the audience in *Medusa*, further along the line of Incandenza's movement toward stasis, does not even need to be lured into its passivity.

*Medusa,* in which "mobile holograms of two visually lethal mythological females duel with reflective surfaces on-stage while a live crowd of spectators turns to stone" (988), further develops this notion of cinematic stasis. As the audience within the film begins to turn to stone, not one person heads for the exit; the spectacle on stage transfixes the audience. They are "rapt and clearly entertained to the gills . . . they keep spontaneously applauding" (397) until they, too, are turned to stone. Shaviro writes that, as film viewers, "we are incited to keep on looking, again and again, precisely because our desire for comprehension and control is never satiated. The more we look, the less we are able to make anything of what we see; we can only abandon ourselves to it" (208). The audiences for *Cage III* and *Medusa* completely abandon themselves to the images they are watching. This abandonment leads to a transformation that happens at an impasse, on the edge of stasis, as the audience loses itself in turning to stone. The audiences within both of these films reach the end of a line as they achieve complete stasis; Incandenza's filmography shows that his movements toward stasis take off in another direction, away from audiences within films and toward actual audiences watching films.

*The Joke* attempts to instantiate stasis in its actual audience by creating a feedback loop in which it statically watches itself moving toward stasis. In this film, Incandenza sets up cameras in the theater that "record the 'film's' audience and project the resultant raster onto screen—the theater audience watching itself watch itself get the obvious 'joke' and become increasingly self-conscious and uncomfortable and hostile supposedly comprises the films involuted 'antinarrative' flow" (988–989). *The Joke* warns its audience that it should stay away from the film. Posters for the movie read "'*THE JOKE*': You Are Strongly Advised NOT to Shell Out Money to See This Film" (397); this warning was taken by the film's audience as "a cleverly ironic anti-ad joke" (397). Regardless, *The Joke* continues projecting its audience onto the screen until the last member leaves the theater, "which ended up being more than maybe twenty minutes only when there were critics or film-academics in the seats, who studied themselves studying themselves taking notes with endless fascination and finally left only when the espresso finally impelled them to the loo" (398). In other words, *The Joke* creates stasis by cultivating this "endless fascination," an inability to look away from a completely boring image. The film becomes completely about the incitement to continue looking; once this incitement is escaped, the film ends. It exists only as long as its audiences' "infinite acceptance" continues; without the stasis of audience passivity, it literally ceases to exist.

Incandenza's *Infinite Jest* continues the movement toward stasis by supposedly being so visually entertaining that viewers immediately become addicted to viewing the film, so addicted that they will die in front of the screen, or go through a withdrawal so severe that it leaves them catatonic if they are forcibly stopped from watching it. This lethal entertainment becomes an object of desire for a group of terrorists, who imagine whole cities "inert, sybaritically entranced, staring, without bodily movement, home-bounded, fouling their divans and . . . chairs" (728). What exactly it is in the film that creates such a profound passivity remains unclear, since anyone viewing it becomes too addicted to escape it long enough to even describe it. At the same time, the novel offers hints that the film consists of two scenes. The first scene involves a veiled woman going through a revolving door and seeing someone she has not seen in a long time. Both characters then continue around in the revolving doors "for several whirls" (939). The second scene consists of the veiled woman looking into a camera that is bolted into a bassinet, and repeatedly apologizing, with "at least twenty minutes of permutations of 'I'm sorry'" (939). This scene is shot with a "wobble" lens meant to simulate the vision of an infant. Whatever the content, the film renders viewers unable to turn away; their eyes become "empty of intent" (508) as they watch the film.

*Infinite Jest* can be read as the culmination of Incandenza's movement toward a stasis that he continually produced in his films, a stasis leading off in various directions and finding its end in his suicide during the postproduction of *Infinite Jest*. His suicide is unclear in motive; no suicide note is left. Until this point, though, Incandenza's production of a decidedly cinematic stasis shows the transformative power of an immobility that can turn one into a giant eyeball or into stone, catch one in a feedback loop of self-referentiality, or cause death through the ultimate "infinite acceptance" of stasis.

## 1. Doctor-Assisted Stasis

Kate Gompert wants to be put into a coma; she tells her doctor, "You could just sedate me for a month. You could do that. All I'd need is I think a month at the outside. Like a controlled coma. You could do that, if you guys want to help" (75). Gompert has just attempted suicide for the third time, but she does not necessarily want to die. And she is not what she calls one of the "self-hating" types who imagine "what everybody'll say at their funeral" (72). Nor were her suicide attempts jokes; she had meant to kill herself. She simply wanted to escape from a causeless, encompassing depression: "I just wanted out" (72). Her suicide attempt was the only way out she could think of. She did not know how to put herself into a coma. She was folded into herself, trapped inside her body by an overwhelming horror. "It's all over everywhere. I don't know what I could call it. It's like I can't get enough outside myself to call it anything" (73). In the Alcoholics Anonymous parlance that Gompert later becomes familiar with, she is trapped in the cage of her self. All she cares about is getting out.

Such a desire is purely pragmatic and has nothing to do with knowledge or understanding. Writing of Kafka's short story "A Report to the Academy," Deleuze and Guattari characterize this desire to escape: "It isn't a question of liberty as against submission, but only a question of a line of escape or, rather, of a simple way out, 'right, left or in any direction,' as long as it is as little signifying as possible" (*Kafka* 6). Of course, Gompert's desire to escape her cage is not identical with Kafka's ape's desire to escape his cage. Both employ different means and encourage different encounters in order to find their way out. Escaping, forging a line of flight, is always a contingent process dependent on surrounding conditions. The ape flees its cage by becoming human; Gompert wants to flee hers by becoming comatose. At the same time, both of these means of escape have nothing to do with signification or meaning.[2]

Gompert's doctor cannot understand her desire for unconsciousness. He keeps asking her questions: "Is the feeling you're explaining something you've experienced in your other depressions, then, Katherine?" (72). The conversation between doctor and patient never connects; the doctor wants to diagnose, but Gompert only wants the doctor to do something, to take some action that will allow her to escape. Knowing that the doctor will refuse to put her in a month-long coma, Gompert asks for shock treatments. Their consultation reaches an impasse at this point. "The doctor was summarizing her choice of treatment-option, as was her right, on her chart . . . He put her get me out of this in quotation marks. He was adding his own post-assessment question, Then what?, when Kate Gompert began weeping for real" (78). The doctor's question "Then what?" implies that Gompert's strategy is temporary at best, a brief delay that does nothing to address her depression. But there is also a kind of pragmatic logic at work in Gompert's desire to be put into a coma. With no way out of her situation, she calls for a complete shutdown, a total stoppage of life. Stasis offers an immediate solution to her problem. It offers no answer to "Then what?" Instead, Gompert's desire for a coma defers any answer into an unforeseeable future. In a sense, the complete shutdown that

Gompert asks her doctor for is a strategy for producing the future, for producing a reemergence in a different time and space. Unable to act in the present moment, Gompert seeks only to flee into the future, with no thought of what that future might be. Her desire for stasis overwhelms any other considerations.

Parts of *Infinite Jest*'s narrative structure mirror Gompert's concern for immediacy. Often in the novel, characters reach breakdown points, they achieve stasis, and the narrative stops dead and picks up elsewhere. After the scene in the hospital ends, *Infinite Jest* does not mention Gompert again for nearly three hundred pages. She then emerges, referred to in passing, at an Alcoholics Anonymous meeting, described as "the shapely but big-time-troubled new girl Kate Gompert—who mostly just stays in her bed in the new women's 5-Woman room when she isn't at meetings, and is on a Suicidality Contract" (361). She is a resident of "Ennet House Drug and Alcohol Recovery House," a halfway house for addicts, where much of the action of *Infinite Jest* takes place. No mention of her breakdown, or of her movement from the hospital to the halfway house, is made. She simply reappears in the narrative. The same thing happens to other characters as well, such as Ken Erdedy and Joelle Van Dyne (see "Waiting Stasis" and "Drugged Stasis" below). These characters reach a point of stasis, disappear from the narrative, and reemerge much later. The novel focuses on the logic of these breakdown points to the temporary exclusion of "Then what?"—of what happens next. Possible causes for these breakdowns are rarely explored. These detailed descriptions of stasis points create a kind of logic: breakdown, disappearance, reemergence.

This logic should not be read as the logic of all stasis, though. As I discuss throughout this chapter, different forms of stasis create their own logics, and move off in any and all directions. Gompert's reemergence, for instance, is followed by another disappearance from the narrative for another three hundred pages. When she next emerges into the narrative, her thoughts return to a consideration of stasis. She thinks of the clinically-diagnosed "psychotic depression," which she refers to as "It," as "a sort of double bind in which any/all of the alternatives we associate with human agency—sitting or standing, doing or resting, speaking or keeping silent, living or dying—are not just unpleasant but literally horrible" (696). In other words, Gompert equates her depression with an inability to move or act in any way whatsoever. Considered this way, her desire for an even deeper stasis—a coma—makes perfect sense as a means of escape from the "double bind" of her depression. She sees the coma functioning as simply a way out, whatever the possible consequences.

A man whom Gompert remembers meeting at a hospital after an earlier suicide attempt exemplifies the strength of this desire for a way out via a complete stoppage. The man had "bonked his head on the cement floor . . . and when he woke up in the E.R. he was depressed beyond all human endurance, and stayed that way" (697). Again, the novel almost trivializes etiology in favor of mapping kinds of stasis. When she had last heard from the man, he was being "evaluated for a radical new type of psychosurgery where they supposedly went in and yanked out your whole limbic system, which is the part of the brain that causes all sentiment and feeling. The man's fondest dream was anhedonia, complete psychic numbing. I.e. death in life" (698)—that is, stasis at any cost.

## 1. Unthinking Stasis

Hal Incandenza is lying on the floor, perhaps experiencing the early stages of marijuana withdrawal. His friend Michael Pemulis comes into the room, and asks Hal, "Thinking?" Hal replies, "The opposite. Thought-prophylaxis" (907). They converse for a few minutes, then Pemulis leaves and Hal continues lying on the floor, in unthinking stasis. Hal's indifference to thought recurs throughout *Infinite Jest*. Early in the novel, readers learn that Hal enjoys smoking marijuana in secret. His pleasure in such secretiveness goes unexamined, though. "He's never given much thought to why. To why he likes it so much" (51). Later, as he is thinking about his family, he cannot decide how he feels about anything. Considering his brother's close relationship with their late father, he thinks, "It occurred to me to wonder why this was so" (957). He does not pursue this thought. Likewise, he thinks about his mother's affair with one of Hal's fellow students: "I hadn't yet been able to identify a strong feeling one way or the other" (957). This thought, also, does not get pursued. The closest Hal comes to examining his motivations and feelings is when he comes to the realization that "inside Hal there's pretty much nothing at all, he knows" (694).

Understanding Hal's unthinking stasis seems impossible. At the same time, *Infinite Jest* claims that Hal is typical of his "generation" in such unthinkingness: "Hal tends to know way less about why he feels certain ways about the objects and pursuits he's devoted to than he does about the objects and pursuits themselves" (54). While this might seem like a condemnation of Hal's generation, *Infinite Jest* itself becomes infected with unthinking stasis, as the passage continues: "It's hard to say for sure whether this is even exceptionally bad, this tendency" (54). Reading the novel, it can become difficult to think about this unthinking stasis, except that it proliferates and forms parts of other kinds of stasis (see especially the sections "Tennis Stasis," "Drugged Stasis," and "Cinematic Stasis" below).

A bird falls into a Jacuzzi, where Hal's brother Orin, a professional football punter, is soaking his sore leg. He does not know what to make of this situation. "He'd just sat there . . . looking at the bird, without a conscious thought in his head" (44). Orin also achieves this thoughtless state on the football field, in the moment before he kicks, when the crowd noise gets so loud that "he literally could not hear himself think out there" (295). Ken Erdedy (see "Waiting Stasis") achieves this unthinking state while waiting for his drug dealer. He realizes that his marijuana addiction is out of control, but he was "unprepared to commit himself to the course of action that would be required to explore the question" (20). Don Gately, involved in a fight, ceases all thought: "If you asked Gately what he was feeling right this second he'd have no idea" (610). *Infinite Jest* points to lots of ways of stopping thought; at the same time, the novel never dwells on these moments, almost as if unthinking stasis repels all thought.

## 1. *M*A*S*H* Stasis

Hugh Steeply's father[3] liked *M*A*S*H*. But his liking for the show transformed into something else; what started as an "an attachment or a habit" (639) quickly became an "obsession" (641). As Steeply retells this story many years later, he makes no attempt to understand why his father became obsessed with the show; rather, he simply details what happened as attachment turned to obsession. His father's obsession began with a refusal to ever miss the show during its weekly network showing. From there he moved on to the daily reruns in syndication; he purchased a

VCR to tape and catalog every episode broadcast. He started to take notes as he watched the show. He quoted snippets of *M*A*S*H* over dinner. Eventually, Steeply's father began sending letters to the show's characters. Finally, he refused to leave his den, where he eventually died.

Steeply's story is summed up by the person to whom he is telling the story, a man named Marathe: "An otherwise harmless U.S.A. broadcast television program took his life, because of the consuming obsession. This is your anecdote" (646). But Marathe summarizes wrongly, as Steeply says, "No. It was a transmural infarction. Blew out the whole ventricle. His whole family had a history: the heart" (646). So, this obsession with *M*A*S*H* does not work as a cautionary tale about the collapse of "crucial distinctions" (643) between fantasy and reality. Steeply's father gained something through his withdrawal from the everyday world of jobs and family; as Marathe says, "The obsessed frequently endure" (646).

Why? What did Steeply's father gain from his obsession? What did the world of *M*A*S*H* do for him? Where did the impasse that he produced "in his easy chair, set at full Recline" (646), take him? His consuming obsession helped him to reach a point where he could reconfigure the world. Not through the passive stasis of the TV watcher, but through the active production of a builder of worlds, Steeply's father builds a world where, in the words of one of *Infinite Jest*'s tennis instructors, he can occur. That is, through an encounter with *M*A*S*H*, Steeply's father carves out a new world within the workaday world he had previously inhabited. In his easy chair, he works with the tools available to slow down one world in order to speed up another. Doing this is, of course, no easy task. For one thing, lots of tools are needed to produce the necessary encounters that will reconfigure time.

Here is what Steeply's father needs: perpetual episodes of *M*A*S*H*, a notebook and pen to "decode" the episodes, an accommodating family, and time, lots of time. In fact, he needs all of his time to bring a *M*A*S*H* world into actuality. Rendering the virtual world of a TV show into a livable space takes hard work and long periods of stillness. Once Steeply's father has enough episodes of *M*A*S*H* available to watch the show continually, he needs an "uncomplaining" (645) wife willing to accommodate his obsession.[4] Then he needs the aforementioned large portions of time to fill "scores of notebooks" with a "secret book" (646) that details the workings of this world, a secret book that decodes "some sort of coded communication to certain viewers about an end to our familiar world-time and the advent of a whole different order of world-time" (644). For instance, "One theory involved the fact, which the old man found extremely significant, that the historical Korean Police Action of the U.N. lasted only roughly two-odd years, but that '$M*A*S*H$' itself was by then into something like its seventh year of new episodes" (644). Noting this incongruity allows Steeply's father to begin to theorize, and then to live by, a new order of time, a time where a faulty heart takes longer than expected to kill him: "The pathologist said it was amazing he'd lasted this long" (646). Unfortunately, not much more can be said about the productive power of Steeply's father's reconfigured world. We don't know what this world produces because we can only glimpse it from the outside. *Infinite Jest* simply does not have the time to provide complete access to Steeply's father's world.[5] After his death, Hugh Steeply reads the notebooks but can make no sense of them. A whole world died with his father. But what is important to note is that this world did not kill him; $M*A*S*H$ stasis reconfigured him and allowed him to live, seemingly stuck in his easy chair.

## 1. Waiting Stasis

Ken Erdedy is waiting for a drug dealer. She's late—"She'd promised to come at one certain time, and it was past that time" (18)—and Erdedy is becoming anxious. His patience grows thin; he watches a bug crawl around on a stereo shelf; he watches TV but can only pay attention for a few seconds at a time. But the promised marijuana is only the beginning of what he is waiting for. Marijuana functions as a catalyst for Erdedy; buying, and smoking, two hundred grams of "unusually good marijuana" (18) will allow Erdedy to "shut the whole system down" (20). He has already gone shopping for supplies, and he has put a message on his answering machine saying that he has been called out of town. As soon as the woman with the marijuana arrives, Erdedy will draw the blinds and hole up in his apartment until he has smoked all two hundred grams. He plans on doing this in four days. He wants to smoke so much so that he can kill the desire for more. "He'd cure himself by excess" (22).

He wants to shut down his life. And he does not know why. In fact, he has no interest in examining why he wants to bring his whole life to a standstill (see "Unthinking Stasis"). He wants to quit smoking so much marijuana, but he has no desire to explore any reasons why he might enjoy falling into a hole for four days: "It occurred to him that he would disappear into a hole in a girder inside him that supported something inside him. He was unsure what the thing inside him was and was unprepared to commit himself to the course of action that would be required to explore the question" (20). There's no deep psychological drama here; it is not as if he wants to die or to escape from any specific horrible aspect of his life. He does not reflect on his past, and the novel offers no reasons why he might be in the state that he is in. He simply wants to stop everything; a complete shutdown is his only concern.

Erdedy has tried this same method to kill his addiction several times before, but it has never worked. Still, he continues his anxious wait. His waiting is interminable, completely functionless. The longer he waits, the less he can do. After four hours of waiting, he is nearly catatonic. Then something happens. The phone and intercom ring at the same time; he cannot make a decision:

> He moved first toward the telephone console, then over toward his intercom module, then convulsively back toward the sounding phone, and then tried somehow to move toward both at once, finally, so that he stood splay-legged, arms wildly out as if something's been flung, splayed, entombed between the two sounds, without a thought in his head. (27)

The chapter ends here, with Erdedy in stasis, unable to move in any direction. Like Kate Gompert after her breakdown (see "Doctor-Assisted Stasis"), Erdedy disappears from *Infinite Jest*'s narrative for nearly three hundred pages, and then emerges as a resident of Ennet House. The time between his disappearance in stasis and his reemergence at the recovery house gets mentioned only in passing; he is described as having "came into the House about a month ago from some cushy Belmont rehab" (360). In other words, readers never learn how Erdedy gets from the immobile space between the sounds of his intercom and telephone to the space of Ennet House. His four-day "holing up" never gets discussed.

Instead, the intervening time between Erdedy's stasis and his reappearance gets glossed over. It is as if his achievement of stasis works as a catalyst, as a point where inaction equals a kind of action. That is, his inability to move creates a means of escape from his marijuana addiction. His reemergence at Ennet House has nothing to do with self-reflection or an understanding of his addiction. Rather, his stillness projects him into the future. While waiting for the drug dealer, he notices an insect crawling on a shelf. The insect stops moving, and it is described as sitting with an "immobility that seemed like the gathering of a force" (24). Likewise, Erdedy's inability to move can be read as a pause before movement, a stoppage that gathers force and then moves off in a different direction. This pause, this waiting, produces a different configuration of time for Erdedy. As he waits, he stares at a clock and notices that what he thought was a single click of the clock moving from one minute to the next is a bit more complex. "The clicks of his portable clock were really composed of three smaller clicks, signifying he supposed preparation, movement, and readjustment" (21). The stasis of waiting functions as a preparation for a movement, a movement that *Infinite Jest* does not describe as it focuses on the frozen moment before movement, and then jumps ahead to the point of reemergence. Waiting stasis brings everything to a complete stop to paradoxically produce an emergence in a different time and space.

## 1. Drug Stasis

*Infinite Jest* claims that there are two types of drug addicts: "Those who like downs and Mr. Hope rarely enjoy stimulants, while coke- and 'drine-fiends as a rule abhor marijuana. This is an area of potentially fruitful study in addictionology" (1053). In a sense, with its close attention to the effects of drugs, *Infinite Jest* is such a study. Elsewhere, the novel describes these two broad categories of drugs as "engine-revvers" and "edge-bevelling" (984), or stimulants and depressants. In other words, drug addiction gets classified, in part, as a way of altering one's relation with time; drugs work as a way of speeding up or slowing down time. A large number of *Infinite Jest*'s endnotes detail the chemistry and effects of various drugs, both legal and illegal, including, among many others, Cimetidine, cocaine, Dilaudid, LSD, MDMA, Seldane, Tenuate, and Xanax. At the same time, the novel focuses in detail on the kinds of stasis reached through four types of drugs: two "engine-revvers," cocaine and DMZ, and two "edge-bevellers," narcotics and marijuana.

On cocaine, Randy Lenz is described as "never sleeping, ever moving, hiding in bright-lit and public plain sight, the last place They would think to find him. . . . The trick, he's found, is not to sleep or eat, to stay up and moving at all times, alert in all six directions at all times" (717). Constant motion makes him invisible. While this might seem like the opposite of stasis, Joelle van Dyne's experience freebasing cocaine shows that this increase in metabolism is itself a kind of stasis. After smoking the drug,

> the 'base frees and condenses, compresses the whole experience to the implosion of one terrible shattering spike in the graph, an afflated orgasm of the heart that makes her feel, truly, attractive, sheltered by limits, deveiled and loved, observed and alone and sufficient and female, full, as if watched for an instant by God. She always sees, after inhaling, right at the apex, at the graph's spike's tip, Bernini's "Ecstasy of St. Teresa," . . . the saint recumbent, half-supine, her flowing stone robe lifted by the angel. (235)

The apex of the high is the ultimate stasis point, a point where the user is both ecstatic and sheltered, outside of the self but still defined. This moment of pure stasis becomes "Too Much Fun" (235) for Joelle; the rest of existence pales in comparison, and she decides to kill herself by overdosing. The stillness within continual motion of the cocaine high is impossible to sustain. The stasis inevitably ends.

The much stronger DMZ, which one character describes as "the Great White Shark of organo-synthesized hallucinogens" (211), is a different story. The stasis achieved through the use of this drug is more intense and longer lasting. The drug's effects are described as "temporally-cerebral and almost ontological . . . whereby the ingester perceives his relation to the ordinary flow of time as radically . . . altered" (170). The DMZ user experiences a kind of stasis way beyond that of other drugs. One character tells of an army convict injected with a massive dose of DMZ in the 1970s, as a military experiment in mind control, who is said to be still sitting "in some impossible lotus position, singing show tunes in a scary deadly-accurate Ethel-Merman-impression voice" (214). Another DMZ user says that after ingesting the drug, he saw the sky, for several weeks, as "a flat square coldly Euclidian grid with black axes and a thread-fine reseau of lines creating grid-type coordinates . . . with the DOW Ticker running up one side of the grid and the NIKEI Index running down the other, and the Time and Celsius Temp to like serious decimal points flashing along the bottom axis of the sky's screen" (542). Both the ticker and time and temperature were correct whenever he checked them against a real clock or newspaper. And there is also "an Italian lithographer who'd ingested DMZ once and made a lithograph comparing himself on DMZ to a piece of like Futurist sculpture, plowing at high knottage through time itself, kinetic even in stasis, plowing temporally ahead, with time coming off him like water in sprays and wakes" (996). This notion of being "kinetic even in stasis" resounds with the description of cocaine producing an effect of complete stillness within unending motion. Such drug use speeds up time for the users in *Infinite Jest,* propelling them toward a complete stoppage that can be achieved no other way.

On the other hand, *Infinite Jest*'s narcotics and marijuana ingesters approach stasis through a continual slowing down of time, a steady approach to complete stillness. In fact, the novel even provides an equation for achieving stasis via "downers": "(Quaalades) + (not even that many beers) = getting whapped by the nearest sidewalk—as in you're walking innocently along down a sidewalk and out of nowhere the sidewalk comes rushing up to meet you: WHAP. Happened time after fucking time" (904–905). Don Gately enacts this equation so much throughout high school that everything else—homework, football practice, class—falls by the wayside. His fondness for this kind of stasis continues. When on depressants, Gately is described as becoming "this totally taciturn withdrawn dead-like person . . . sitting for hours real low in his canvas chair, practically lying in this chair whose canvas bulged and legs bowed out, speaking barely at all" (893). In contrast, he is described as "a great and cheerful stand-up jolly-type guy off the nod" (893). Nevertheless, his desire for the complete stoppage produced by depressants comes to rule his life.

He begins injecting narcotics to slow time down even more. When he injected drugs, "you'd have to almost pry his chin off his chest. Kite used to say it was like Gately shot cement instead of narcotics" (893). Gately continues in this movement toward infinite slowness, which culminates in a days-long binge on Dilaudid. Toward the end of the binge, "Gately felt less high than disembodied. It was obscenely pleasant. His head left his shoulders" (981), and he passed out, having brought all movement to a complete stop.

While various drug-induced stasis points are considered throughout *Infinite Jest*, marijuana-induced stasis gets the closest scrutiny in the novel. Indeed, "Marijuana Thinking" gets defined in detail, and many examples of such thought populate the novel:

> This tendency to involuted abstraction is sometimes called "Marijuana Thinking"; and by the way, the so-called "Amotivational Syndrome" consequent to massive Bob Hope-consumption is a misnomer, for it is not that Bob Hope-smokers lose interest in practical functioning, but rather Marijuana-Think themselves into labyrinths of reflexive abstraction that seem to cast doubt on the very possibility of practical functioning, and the mental labor of finding one's way out consumes all available attention and makes the Bob Hope-smoker look physically torpid and apathetic and amotivated sitting there, when really he is trying to claw his way out of a labyrinth. (1048)

Hal Incandenza is often afflicted with such thinking. At one point, he contemplates the complications that could result from asking a simple question: "I could see me asking him where he'd been all week leading to so many different possible responses and further questions that the prospect was almost overwhelming, so enervating I could barely get out that I'd just been lying here on the floor" (907). At another point, Hal gets paralyzed with absorption, and the "almost infinite-seeming implications" (341) of the situation leave him unable to act.

*Infinite Jest* posits that there is no way out of this stasis, because attempts by the heavy user to quit smoking only intensifies the stasis of "Marijuana Thinking": "The increasing emotional abstraction, poverty of affect, and then total emotional catalepsy— the obsessive analyzing, finally the paralytic stasis that results from the obsessive analysis of all possible implications of both getting up from the couch and not getting up from the couch" (503). The addict becomes trapped in perpetual stasis, able neither to get up from the couch nor to remain on it.

## 1. Wraith Stasis

James Incandenza is dead. Don Gately, because of a gunshot wound, is in and out of consciousness. He cannot decide if he is awake or dreaming, or even dreaming within a dream. Regardless, toward the end of *Infinite Jest,* Incandenza appears as a "ghostish figure" (829) in Gately's hospital room. Gately attempts to ascribe meanings to the wraith's visitation. He wonders if the wraith is a representation of kids that Gately picked on as a child who have come back to haunt him, but the wraith says that he is "nothing of the sort" (829) and that he has "no sort of grudge or agenda" (829). Gately then thinks that maybe the wraith "could be a sort of epiphanyish visitation from Gately's personally confused understanding of God, a Higher Power or something" (833), but "the wraith smiles sadly and says something like Don't we both wish" (833). He also considers that the wraith might represent "the Disease" of Gately's addiction, "exploiting the loose security of Gately's fever-addled mind" (833), but the wraith makes it clear that this is not the case, either. In other words, the wraith insists that he has nothing to do with Gately's past or even with the inner workings of his mind or his struggle with addiction.

As he communicates with the wraith, Gately tries to figure out exactly what state of consciousness he is in, but Incandenza, who has described himself to Gately as "just a generic garden-variety wraith" (829), tells Gately not to bother with such issues. "The wraith made a weary morose gesture as if not wanting to bother to get into any sort of confusing dream-v.-real controversies. The wraith said Gately might as well stop trying to figure it out and just capitalize on its presence" (830). In other words, the wraith says to Gately, Don't ask me what I am or why I'm here, just focus on what I can do for you.

The wraith notes that they can converse without speaking, which benefits Gately because he has a tube in his throat. Beyond this fact, though, the wraith's purpose in communicating with Gately is not clear, especially considering the difficulty involved in the communication. The wraith tells him how difficult it is for wraiths to communicate with humans, as wraiths "exist . . . in a totally different Heisenbergian dimension of rate-change and time-passage [so that] normal animate men's actions and motions look, to a wraith, to be occurring at about the rate a clock's hour-hand moves, and are just as interesting to look at" (831). In other words, normal human time and space look incredibly static to a wraith. And conversely, for a human to see a wraith, the wraith must stay immobile for long periods of time.

The wraith says that he has been sitting "still as a root, in the chair by Gately's bedside for the wraith equivalent of three weeks" (836) so that he can communicate with Gately. In other words, stasis is relative, and it also serves as a means of reordering time and space. It is only through an incredibly long stasis that the wraith can move between his experience of time and space and Gately's human experience of the same.

The wraith notes the incredible difficulty of achieving such stasis, which prompts Gately to consider why the wraith wants to communicate with him. Gately did not know Incandenza when he was alive, and since the wraith spends the bulk of the conversation talking about Hal, Gately does not know why the wraith is talking to him instead of "holding very still for wraith-months and trying to have an interface with the fucking son" (840, italics in the original). *Infinite Jest* never establishes exactly why the wraith communicates with Gately, but the main reason seems to be Gately's immobility; as the wraith sits completely static for three weeks of his time, he knows that Gately will likewise be unmoving in his hospital bed. Still, Gately's thought that the wraith should haunt his son brings up connections to *Hamlet,* and particularly to the role of the ghost of Hamlet's father.[6]

One could argue that the ghost of Hamlet's father clearly sets Hamlet on the path to revenge that drives the entire narrative of the play. Hamlet's father's ghost makes something happen, even as Hamlet continually breaks down and reaches various impasses on his way to revenge. But James Incandenza's ghost serves no such narrative purpose. For one thing, he never appears to his son Hal; instead, Incandenza haunts a man he did not even know while alive. Also, the novel ends with Gately still in a semiconscious state, his fate unknown. In fact, the main similarity between the appearance of father-ghosts in *Hamlet* and *Infinite Jest* is quite tenuous. At roughly the same time Incandenza is haunting Gately, Hal has a fleeting thought about Hamlet: "It's always seemed a little preposterous that Hamlet, for all his paralyzing doubt about everything, never once doubts the reality of the ghost" (900). This thought paralyzes Hal, so that "just the thought of getting up made me glad I was lying on the floor" (900). *Infinite Jest*'s first chapter—which occurs last chronologically—suggests that Hal, over a year later, remains in stasis, emotionally paralyzed to the point where he is incapable of speech. The wraith, the ghost of Hal's father, produces no action; he makes no attempt to communicate with Hal, to help him overcome his paralyzing stasis.

## 1. Infinite Stasis

The unnamed speaker of "B.I. 59," one of the many such "interviews" in Wallace's 1999 collection of short stories, *Brief Interviews with Hideous Men,* is institutionalized because he has vaguely defined problems regarding control and the ability to act, or to "exercise again true power of any type" (185), which the interview only mentions in passing. In fact, most details are scant throughout the interview. Readers never learn exactly why the man is institutionalized. The interviewer's identity is not given, although, given the setting, the questioner could be taken to be a therapist. Even the questions are not known to the reader; they are marked only by the letter "Q," which serves as a stand-in for the questions to which the speaker is responding. While the speaker spends the bulk of the interview remembering his childhood, he does not provide the typical details. We learn that the speaker is the child of a Soviet mathematician who moved the family frequently from military post to post, and that he spent many of his days in "State Exercise Facilities" where he would read while his mother and brother exercised. The speaker describes himself as "a weak, unathletic, and somewhat sickly adolescent, a scholarly and dreamy youth . . . of nervous constitution and little confidence or social outgoingness" (182). The speaker does not focus on this family dynamic during the interview. Instead, the bulk of his narrative is a detailed description of a childhood erotic fantasy involving the production of stasis that may or may not be the cause of his present condition.

The speaker remembers that "I experienced my first erotic sensations" (181) while watching the television show *Bewitched.* From this first experience, he remembers trying to create an infinitely detailed fantasy of stasis that eventually causes him to have a mental breakdown. One particular aspect of *Bewitched* relates to his fantasy:

> The protagonist, Elizabeth Montgomery, would perform a circular motion with her hand, accompanied by the sound of a zither or harp, and produce a supernatural effect in which all motion ceased and all the television program's other characters suddenly were frozen in mid-gesture and were oblivious and rigid, lacking all animation. (181)

The speaker describes his fantasy, which takes place in the State Exercise Facility, as having consisted of two parts: (1) he could, with "a highly concentrated gaze . . . directed at the woman who was the object of it, renders her irresistibly attracted toward me" (183–184); (2) he could, then, with the same circular hand gesture as Elizabeth Montgomery's, "cause all motion and activity in the State Exercise Facility to cease" (184). In his fantasy, he would then, with the woman he has entranced, "copulat[e] in variations of sexual frenzy upon an exercise mat in the room's center" (184).

As he continues through his youth with this fantasy, he discovers a logical problem that "demanded a resolution consistent with the enframing logic of the hand's powers" (185). As the son of a mathematician, the speaker notes that "I was responsible" (185) for solving the logical inconsistency. In short, he comes to realize that, for his fantasy to make sense, he must freeze time and space not only within the State Exercise Facility but also within the whole military post, so that no one from outside could enter the spatial and temporal stasis of the facility. The speaker extends this logic to the realization that he must also, within his fantasy, freeze "the entire state" (187), and then "the very world's entire population itself" (188). He takes ill with this responsibility and spends days in bed with "the labor of imagination of constructing a sufficiently motionless and atemporal planet earth" (189). His logic then expands from the world to the solar system, to the Milky Way Galaxy, to the galaxies it orbits, to the whole universe.

He actually begins "research and calculations" (190) that would make this infinite stasis mathematically logical. When he realizes, after "many months" (190) of work, that he has made an oversight in his calculations—they had been based upon data that calculated from "an earth . . . in the naturally, unfrozen everchanging mode of reality, and that all of it therefore must be recalculated from my fantasy's gesture's theoretical haltings of the earth and neighboring satellites" (190–191)—he breaks down: "It was then I broke down from it. The fantasy's single gesture of one adolescent hand had proven to entail an infinitely complex responsibility more befitting of a God than a mere boy . . . It was at this moment I renounced, resigned, became again merely a sickly and unconfident youth" (191). In other words, he breaks down at the point where he realizes that the small space and time of stasis he fantasized producing in the State Exercise Facility has spun completely out of his control. He finds it impossible to make the infinite calculations that would be necessary to represent a logically coherent static universe. He makes "the reversing gesture of linked circles" that "opened swiftly out to include all known bodies in motion" (191). The infinite connections that would create a unified fantasy are theoretically impossible. Infinite stasis cannot be thought.

## 1. Tennis Stasis

One of James Incandenza's films, a "documentary history" (986) of tennis, is called *Flux in a Box.* For the students at Enfield Tennis Academy, tennis becomes a way of life, a movement toward a static, infinite world circumscribed by the lines of the tennis court. The tennis instructors at Enfield view their jobs as providing students with access to what instructor Gerhard Schtitt describes as a "sheltering second world inside the lines" (459). As Schtitt explains to his students, the whole purpose of practicing and playing tennis is "to make for you this second world that is always the same: there is in this world you, and in the hand a tool, there is a ball, there is opponent with his tool, and always only two of you, you and this other, inside the lines, with always a purpose to keep this world alive" (459). The whole purpose of tennis is to keep the space between the lines of the court "always the same," infinitely unchanging.

Schtitt's formula for achieving this total access to the static world of the tennis court is to "disappear inside the game: break through limits: transcend: improve: win" (84). The way to achieve this disappearance is through unending repetition so that you reach the stage where "the point of repetition is there is no point" (118). Such repetition makes play almost unconscious, so that "you're barely involved" (166), "playing with such ease and total mindless effortless effort and entranced concentration you don't even stop to consider whether to run down every ball" (166). As Schtitt explains it to the players, "You have a chance to occur, playing" (459). "Occurring" equals being fully in the "second world" of the tennis court, "removed, for a moment, from the connectedness of all events" (96). But the complete shutdown of the world outside the tennis court is difficult to maintain.

Hal Incandenza, narrating a film his brother has made about tennis, *Tennis and the Feral Prodigy,* says, "Here is how to avoid thinking about any of this by practicing and playing until everything runs on autopilot and talent's unconscious exercise becomes a way to escape yourself, a long waking dream of pure play" (173). But this stasis of "pure play" is hard to reach and can easily be lost. After a poor game, a coach tells Hal, "You just never quite occurred out there, kid" (686)—a statement that greatly upsets Hal: "His choice of words chills Hal to the root" (686). He knows that he has fallen out of tennis stasis, that he has momentarily lost the ability "to occur," to enter into the infinitely static world of the tennis court.

## 1. Heroic Stasis

At a college admissions meeting at the University of Arizona, Hal Incandenza has been coached not to move or say anything, to "err on the side of neutrality and not attempt what would feel to me like a pleasant expression or smile" (3). As the meeting continues, Hal sits mutely; thinking that he may have made an expression, he does what he describes as "the safe thing," "relaxing every muscle in my face, emptying out all expression" (5). This meeting takes place in the first chapter of *Infinite Jest*, a chapter that is chronologically last in the novel's time frame. The reason why Hal has been coached to remain silent is not completely clear: he may have watched the lethally entertaining film made by his late father; he may have swallowed the potent drug DMZ; he may be in serious marijuana withdrawal. As the meeting continues, Hal attempts to "expend energy on remaining utterly silent in my chair, empty, my eyes two great pale zeros" (8). When he is forced to speak, the various deans at the meeting think that he is having a seizure. Hal says, "I am not what you see and hear" (13); what they hear and see is "*sub*animalistic noises and sounds" (14, italics in the original) and "flailing" (14), "like a time-lapse, a flutter of some sort of awful . . . growth" (14). He is rushed off to a hospital; in the ambulance he notes that "there are, by the *O.E.D. VI*'s count, nineteen nonarchaic synonyms for *unresponsive*" (17).

The cause of Hal's seizure, along with the reasons he cannot communicate, remains unclear. At the same time, his desire to remain perfectly still resonates with the way he has been taught to play tennis—"let everything bounce off you; do nothing" (9) (see "Tennis Stasis" above)—and one of the application essays he has submitted to the university. Among the nine essays he submitted is one called "The Emergence of Heroic Stasis in Broadcast Entertainment" (7). The text of this essay appears later in the novel. In the essay, Hal argues that television drama has progressed from the "classically modern hero of action," exemplified by Chief Steve McGarret of the 1970s series *Hawaii Five-O*, to the postmodern "hero of reaction" (141), exemplified by Captain Frank Furillo of the 1980s series *Hill Street Blues*. Hal ends his essay with a gesture toward the future of television heroes:

> But what comes next? What North American hero can hope to succeed the placid Frank? We await, I predict, the hero of non-action, the catatonic hero, the one beyond calm, divorced from all stimulus, carried here and there across sets by burly extras whose blood sings with retrograde amines. (142)

The kinds of stasis produced in *Infinite Jest* can be read as movements toward this heroic stasis. Hal Incandenza, Don Gately, James O. Incandenza, Kate Gompert, Ken Erdedy, Hugh Steeply's father, and Joelle van Dyne all employ various strategies to achieve "nonaction" and reach a stasis point, to shut off all movement. Compiling these attempts to achieve stasis leads to its own stoppage in an asignifying stasis.

## $n - 1$. Asignifying Stasis

A catalog of kinds of stasis in David Foster Wallace could go on and on, from the stasis of "the static, momentumless music" (450) that resounds through *Infinite Jest* to the stasis of "Extralinear Dynamics," the form of math whose "theorems and nonexistent proofs amount to extremely lucid and elegant admissions of defeat in certain cases, hands thrown up w/ complete deductive justification" (994), to catatonic stasis, the stasis of seizures, withdrawal stasis, the stasis of the recovery movement. *Infinite Jest* can be read as containing infinite means of achieving stasis; the act of reading—the physical impossibility and time constraints that prevent cataloging everything—sets the limits of what can be done. There are "n" kinds of stasis in Wallace's fiction; the above cataloging is an attempt to break down the unity of signifying stasis that I refer to above, to create a line of flight that escapes literary criticism's drive to produce unity.

What is wrong with signification and unity? What is productive about breaking it down? Deleuze and Guattari write that "the notion of unity appears only when there is a power takeover in the multiplicity by the signifier or a corresponding subjectification proceeding" (*Thousand* 8). This "power takeover . . . by the signifier" happens when literary criticism seeks a complete understanding of a work of a fiction, a point from which everything can be understood. In the case of *Infinite Jest,* one could locate this "takeover," as Hayles does, on *Infinite Jest*'s recursive loops that allow us to see "the underlying ideologies driving" ("Illusion" 695) the world. That is, at root, the seemingly endless recursive loops of the novel find their meaning as criticism reveals their base structure. They all revolve around a unifying sign.

Likewise, "subjectification proceeding[s]" seek unity on the level of the subject. Following this logic, a character stuck in stasis must be lacking something. In the case of *Infinite Jest*'s characters, the underlying signification of stasis can be found in their "childhood roots (*'radicalis'*)" (LeClair 14). In both cases, criticism seeks out an underlying, unifying point in order to render fiction as a reflection of the world, as an "imitative form of the world" (LeClair 16) that can tell us what fiction means, but nothing of what it can do. Unity gets to the bottom of things, prevents any sort of action except the reconstitution of a subject, even when pointing out the dangers of that subject, as Hayles does in her reading of the political implications of *Infinite Jest:*

> *Infinite Jest* suggests a more constructive approach when it shows that the idea of an autonomous liberal subject can be a recipe for disaster in a world densely interconnected with interlocking complex systems. Authenticity in this vision is not about escaping from the realm of the social, but rather about recognizing the profound interconnections that bind us all together, human actors and nonhuman life forms, intelligent machines and intelligent people. We escape from Entertainment not by going to the woods but by recognizing our responsibilities to one another. ("Illusion" 696)

Reading here becomes an act of self-recognition that reconstitutes the subject not as autonomous, but as complex liberal, so that the subject chooses to see that "I" cannot escape the social. The complex liberal subject is the one who reads *Infinite Jest* and proclaims, "I now see myself as part of the complex world that this book represents. I had better reconsider the ways that I act in the world."

A reading that moves toward an asignifying stasis involves more than self-recognition. Following Deleuze and Guattari, I want to argue that reading should seek to "lengthen, prolong, and relay the line of flight; make it vary, until you have produced the most abstract and tortuous of lines of $n$ dimensions and broken directions" (*Thousand* 11). In this chapter, I have attempted to do this by mapping the dimensions of kinds of stasis in Wallace. Wallace's fiction continually provides detailed descriptions of breakdowns and stasis, but then jumps to another plane, never quite offering a way to interpret the movement toward stasis, never getting down to any roots, and never unifying the kinds of stasis that it produces. Stasis becomes that which is open ended and resistant to unification. The achievement of stasis in Wallace is always the singular moment when something is happening, when experiences of time and space are being altered via access to infinite speed and infinite slowness. In these singular moments, I read the emergence of what Guattari calls "mutant" (18) forms of subjectivity. Such mutations get created through "a rupture of sense, a cut, a fragmentation, the detachment of a semiotic content"(18). Responding to these "mutant" subjectivities seems to be an ethical matter.

An ethical reading of Wallace might flee the unity of signification and subjectivity that leads toward a unified, even if complex, subject that is often located at the center of the act of reading. As tennis instructor Schtitt claims, "Real tennis was really about . . . not-order, limit, the places where things broke down, fragmented into beauty" (*Infinite* 81). In a similar way, reading too can be about limits, about the breakdowns in representation that lead to new configurations of subjectivity. Moving toward stasis in Wallace's fiction is to undergo transformation. Stasis alters consciousness and provides a way out of a subjectivity that has become too much to bear. As the sheer variety of kinds of stasis shows, the production of stasis is always local. Every breakdown is unique, and every breakdown gets assembled from its own components, be they tennis rackets and court lines, movies, drugs, television shows, fantasies, comas, or novels and literary criticism. Stasis points are points of subjectification that are not reducible to a root or unifiable to a world picture.

Producing an asignifying stasis involves subtracting kinds of stasis from Wallace's fiction and forging new connections rather than relying on the idea that every point is connected to every other point in a final, even if complex, unity. Deleuze and Guattari write, "Flat multiplicities of n dimensions are asignifying and asubjective" (*Thousand* 9). "Kinds of Stasis in David Foster Wallace" is an attempt to produce just such a flat multiplicity, a continuing series of breakdowns, always starting over again at *n*, and not leading toward a coherent whole. This continuing practice of subtracting from the infinite stands in marked contrast to conceptions of fiction as a "narrative ecology."

Arguments that fiction is a narrative ecology rely on a sort of critical distance, a perspective from outside that takes in the whole picture in order to render the narrative whole. Deleuze and Guattari write that "unity always operates in an empty dimension supplementary to that of the system considered (over-coding)" (*Thousand* 8). The critical article functions as an impossible point of control that does not consider the experience of reading or the experience of writing about the novel as a part of the ecology; that considers itself disconnected from its own logic about connectedness and complexity; that ignores the idea that all variables in a complex ecology can never be mapped, as the narrator of "Brief Interview #59" realizes when his fantasy of control itself spins out of control (see "Infinite Stasis" above). In other words, when fiction gets read as a narrative ecology, complexity all too often becomes a synonym for unity, and once unity is found, self-recognition can happen. And then fiction, through a representation of a possible future, can warn us to flee the path of impending ecological disaster.

One might easily argue that the realm of science is better equipped than literature to provide such warnings. I do not necessarily want to make that argument; instead I want to end by pointing to another way of considering the productive force of reading fiction. Instead of an act of self-recognition, reading can provide access to an asignifying world populated by subjectivities that are continually reconfiguring their experiences of time and space. In this reconfiguration, the future is not a unity to be determined, but a series of singular events to be produced. Reading Wallace can be a movement toward a stasis that is a breakdown, not an escape from ecological or social connections (for what would that mean?), but an escape from the recursive loop of self-recognition that enables literary criticism to create unity. Reading, as a movement toward an asignifying stasis, is the ethical cultivation of other connections that bring things to a complete stop, a pause, before starting again somewhere else, staggering around and around, leading in any direction whatsoever. Stopping. Starting. Stopping. Ad infinitum.

# CHAPTER 4

# SILENCE JUNKIES: IRVINE WELSH'S NOVEL SUBJECTIVITIES

*Psychology's mistake was to treat forgetting as a negative determination, not to discover its active and positive character.*

—*Gilles Deleuze*, Nietzsche and Philosophy *(113)*

*The context of our analysis thus has to be the very unfolding of life itself, the process of the constitution of the world, of history. The analysis must be proposed not through ideal forms but within the dense complex of experience.*

—*Michael Hardt and Antonio Negri*, Empire *(30)*

I begin this chapter not in silence, but with two calls for silence from two disparate places, Maurice Blanchot's *Space of Literature* and Irvine Welsh's *Trainspotting*. Blanchot writes that "to write is to make oneself the echo of what cannot cease speaking—and since it cannot, in order to become its echo I have, in a way, to silence it" (*Space* 27). Mark Renton, a character in Welsh's *Trainspotting*, says, "Sometimes ah think that people become junkies just because they subconsciously crave a wee bit ay silence" (7). At first glance, both of these calls for silence appear as refutations of the world, as refusals to engage otherness in any form. Blanchot writes of the writer's necessary "refusal to take part in the world" ("Literature" 315). A character in *Trainspotting* says, "The outside world means fuck all tae us" (87). Both Blanchot's writer and Welsh's junky strive for an all-encompassing silence, a complete shutdown of any and all forms of exteriority. Yet, if one reads Blanchot and Welsh through the murmur of Deleuze, it is precisely this desire to cut off the world that leads to a means of engagement with the world's otherness.

Blanchot's call for silence, read alongside Deleuze's, configures silence not as a revelation of being's essence, but as a space of emergence where subjectivities get produced. This space of emergence bears similarities to the space of reading that I discuss in Chapter 1, to the space of fascinated disgust in Chapter 2, and to the stasis of David Foster Wallace's fiction that I consider in Chapter 3. It is important to note, though, that these spaces are not identical. Each is assembled from different components, and each produces its own singular forms of subjectivity. As I have been arguing, responding to these subjectivities without reducing them to failures or fragments of a missing unity is the ethical work of postmodern literary criticism. In Welsh's case, his characters strive for a total silence. This struggle to find silence is the struggle to produce novel—in both senses of the word—forms of subjectivity: new forms of subjectivity and forms of subjectivity that live on the pages of Welsh's fiction. Welsh's characters resist traditional psychological, sociological, and political narratives of identity formation. In this chapter, I will trace the emergence of these subjectivities and attempt to open a space in postmodern literary criticism where a Welshian subjectivity can emerge into the discourse of postmodern literary criticism and be considered neither as a failure to achieve coherence nor as a simple critique of the contemporary world, but as a new way of living in the world.

## The Writer's Silence

One can only approach Blanchot's space of essential solitude through silence, through a sloughing off of the first person and of time itself. In turn, this very silencing must be forgotten and silenced. For Blanchot, the writer must find a place where the world has been silenced and all that remains is "the indeterminate They, the immense, faceless Someone" (*Space* 33). The writer effaces himself or herself before this faceless "Someone" and affirms "the pure passivity of being" (27). Such an affirmation, though, remains indeterminate. The writer cannot affirm a connection to the world, to otherness, because the faceless "Someone," the impersonal, is "that which prevents, precedes, and dissolves the possibility of any personal relation" (31). The only way to face the impersonal is through effacement. The writer's silent affirmation affirms nothing: "an affirmation in which nothing is affirmed, in which nothing never ceases to affirm itself with the exhausting insistence of the indefinite" (30). Such an affirmation appears as impossible, even negative, work. Blanchot writes, "For it is as if there were no being, except through the loss of being when being lacks" (30). The writer encounters being only in its absence, as something that disappears in its very appearance, as "the absence one sees because it is blinding" (33).

The silent space inhabited by the writer seems to have little or no connection to an ethics of literary criticism, to an engagement, in the world, of the world created in literature. That is, this space hardly seems to call for any sort of response on the part of a reader. Stephen Adam Schwartz writes that "literature, for Blanchot, will become just the sort of sovereign destructive force that puts the world in brackets in order to bring forth its incommunicable 'essence' and origin" (21). Literature, in this reading, serves only to reveal the essential absence at the heart of being; the writer's silent affirmation can be seen as an affirmation of being as a lack. Literature uncovers the impossibility of full self-presence. Paul de Man reads Blanchot in this way. He writes that, for Blanchot,

> criticism thus becomes a form of demystification on the ontological level that confirms the existence of a fundamental distance at the heart of all human experience . . . . Blanchot does not seem to believe that the movement of a poetic consciousness could ever lead us to assert our ontological insight in a positive way. The center always remains hidden and out of reach; we are separated from it by the very substance of time, and we never cease to know that this is the case. (*Blindness* 76–77)

De Man sees a circular criticism emerging from Blanchot. The writer loses himself or herself in the face of the absence at the heart of being; this absence, in turn, always returns the writer to himself or herself. "In his interpretative quest, the writer frees himself from empirical concerns, but he remains a self that must reflect on its own situation . . . He can only do this by 'reading' himself, by turning his conscious attention toward himself, and not toward a forever unreachable form of being" (78). In turning away from the blinding absence of being's lack, the writer returns to his or her self; the writer's silent affirmation turns inward, toward the self and away from the world. For de Man, Blanchot's writings on literature are wholly about the impossibility of criticism. "In his critical work, this theoretician of interpretation prefers to describe the act of interpretation rather than the interpreted insight" (77). In writing about literature, Blanchot can only write about writing about literature in an endless reflective process that inevitably produces a lacking being. In writing about Blanchot writing about literature, the literary critic, in turn, can only produce more and more ever receding readings of the lack at the heart of being. "The absence one sees because it is blinding" is endlessly revealed.

Such a reading ignores the singular power of the writer's silence, a singularity that Blanchot understatedly calls a writer's "tone":

> When we admire the tone of a work . . . [we are] referring to . . . this silence precisely, this vigorous force by which the writer, having been deprived of himself, having renounced himself, has in this effacement nevertheless maintained the authority of a certain power: the power decisively to be still, so that in this silence what speaks without beginning or end might take on form, coherence, and sense. (*Space* 27)

The "vigorous force" of the writer's passivity, what can be called the writer's vigorous passivity, can break the impasse of a de Manian reading of Blanchot. The power that the writer retains through his or her effacement is precisely the ability to say anything at all, to flee from endless repetitions of a fundamental lack. As Blanchot writes, something emerges from a writer's silent effacement that "might take on form, coherence, and sense" (*Space* 27) More than a negative affirmation takes place here. Through tone, a writer produces a work that "contains . . . a content" (28). This "content," the writer's work, is not an expression of the writer's personality, or even a residue of his or her effaced self. Blanchot warns, "A writer cannot withdraw into himself, for he would then have to give up writing" ("Literature" 307). Rather, the content that a writer expresses can be viewed as the product of a unique encounter, where "what is most singular about him and farthest removed from existence as already revealed now reveals itself within shared existence" (307). The work, something written, emerges from a writer's encounter with solitude.[1]

The essential solitude, the silent effacement of the writer, is always populated by encounters. Following Blanchot, Deleuze writes,

> When you work, you are necessarily in absolute solitude . . . But it is an extremely populous solitude. Populated not with dreams, phantasms or plans, but with encounters. An encounter is perhaps the same thing as a becoming, or nuptials. It is from the depth of this solitude that you can make any encounter whatsoever. You encounter people (and sometimes without knowing them or ever having seen them) but also movements, ideas, events, entities. (Deleuze and Parnet 6)

The "essentialness" of the essential solitude is not the revelation of being's lack, but the possibility of becoming that emerges from the essential solitude. The incessant murmur of being that Blanchot writes of is the noise of a becoming that is always at work. A writer emerges from his or her solitude somewhere else; writing is a becoming, not a static process of documenting the blindness of an absence at the heart of the world. To write is to become something other. Deleuze writes, "The writer returns from what he has seen and heard with bloodshot eyes and pierced eardrums" ("Literature" 3). The writer returns from solitude in writing and through writing, and emerges somewhere completely different. Emerging from silence, a writer's content documents his or her singular becoming.

Criticism must respond to this singular becoming through a becoming of its own. It must encounter literature in absolute solitude, not to separate literature and the world, but to connect literature to life, to draw attention to the becomings at work in the act of reading. Literature—encountered through reading and writing—does not reflect life, but it opens a site of becoming that reconfigures and creates life. Careful attention to Welsh's tone and to the space that it emerges from can illustrate criticism's role in the production of novel subjectivities.

## New Scottish Writing and "the Queen's fuckin English"

In Welsh's short story "The Rosewell Incident," a group of aliens intent on taking over Earth set down in Edinburgh. In short order, the aliens adopt the language of a typical Welshian character, Mikey Devlin, who is willing to instruct the aliens in the ways of Earth, "wanted as he was by local police on Earth for a wounding offence at Waverley Station after a full-scale pagger" (192). When the aliens address the world's leaders, translation, as in most science fictions of the "aliens taking over Earth" variety, becomes a problem. But the problem is not that the earthlings cannot understand an extraterrestrial language; rather, the leaders of the world cannot understand the aliens' Edinburgh-inflected speech: "We could fuckin annihilate youse in a swedge. Nae fuckin problem. We've goat the fuckin technology, eh. And the fuckin willpower. So the wey we see is, youse cunts dae as yis ur fuckin well telt and that's it. Endy fuckin story" (216).

This scene seems particularly relevant in general relation to recent developments in Scottish literature and politics and in specific relation to Welsh's place within this emergence. As Andrew Ross writes, because of the successful devolution vote, "Scotland is once again a blip on the radar screen of the 'international community.' Its fledgling parliament is regularly cited as a regional symptom of a new global order, good or bad, depending on the speaker's viewpoint" (83). Hand in hand with this political emergence into the "international community" comes a new Scottish writing, an "extraordinary boom now taking place in Scottish literature" (Ritchie 2), championed by such anthologies as *The Vintage Book of Contemporary Scottish Fiction, Children of Albion Rovers: New Scottish Writing,* and *Acid Plaid: New Scottish Writing,*[2] all of which include selections from Welsh. The *Vintage* anthology, by far the most staid of these collections, draws a connection between this new writing and the sense of new political awareness in Scotland. "For the first time in centuries of insecurity and strife, Scotland has begun to stop defining itself by what it is not—England—and is with good humour facing up to what it is, both bad and good. Future generations will applaud the contribution which the writers in this anthology played in this process" (Kravitz xxxvi). What exactly the role of a "new" Scottish literature is in the formation of a "new" Scotland remains to be determined. Harry Ritchie, the editor of *Acid Plaid,* strikes a more skeptical note on the relation between politics and literature, as he writes that "claims that the wonderful upsurge in Scottish writing has somehow been propelled by the political Zeitgeist . . . lacks anything that vaguely resembles research or evidence" (3). While the relation between what literature and politics in Scotland may be, or become in the future, remains open to debate, one consensus can be noted: Welsh's fiction, particularly *Trainspotting*, has a central role on both the literary and political stage in the world production of Scottish subjectivities.

The back-cover copy of *Acid Plaid* notes Welsh's literary centrality: "Ever since the huge success of Irvine Welsh's *Trainspotting* made Edinburgh the hottest literary scene on the map, there has been a palpable sense that the so-called Scottish Beats have something new, something young and raw and energetic and exciting, to inject into literary culture." Likewise, in his introduction to *Children of Albion Rovers,* Kevin Williamson compares the selection process for the anthology to "picking a [football] team" (1). Welsh becomes Williamson's goalie: "Irvine Welsh—a keeper of the faith [who has] learnt how to cope with the pressure—and the vagaries of the press—producing performances the fans just rave about" (3). The political role of Welsh's fiction, while more difficult to gauge, is also readily apparent. Chris Mitchell argues that *Trainspotting,* with its overt scenes of heroin use, has changed the discourse on drugs in Britain: "The phenomenal success of the film and Irvine Welsh's novel of the same name brought the realities and reasons for drug use into the mainstream for the first time" (par. 3). More concretely, Peter Kravitz, in the introduction to the *Vintage* anthology, points to the "colonised by wankers" rant in *Trainspotting,* and notes that "the Scottish National Party used this monologue by Renton for a recruitment form in September 1996. The Commission for Racial Equality received a complaint about it from a Labour Member of Parliament and it was referred to a lawyer who said that it might be in contravention of the Malicious Publications Act" (xxxii). In his essay on Scottish identity, Angus Calder also focuses on just this speech:

> Fuckin failures in a country ay failures. It's nae good blamin it oan the English fir colonising us. Ah don't hate the English. They're just wankers. We are colonised by wankers. We can't even pick a decent, vibrant, healthy, culture to be colonised by. No. We're ruled by effete assholes. What does that make us? The lowest of the fuckin low, the scum of the earth. The most wretched, servile, miserable, pathetic trash that was ever shat intae creation. Ah don't hate the English. They just git oan wi the shite thuv goat. Ah hate the Scots. (Welsh, *Trainspotting* 78)

Calder notes that in the novel, this monologue takes place as the inner thoughts of Mark Renton, as he sits in an Edinburgh bar with the violent and racist Frank Begbie. In the film, however, the setting changes to "Beautiful Highland Scenery," where one of Renton's friends has "led a small crew of Leith druggies" (219). As the crew refuses to climb around in the countryside, Renton lets fly his rant. Calder argues that the switch of locale here politicizes what might otherwise be "a film decoded without reference to Scotland or to politics" (237). Instead, the scene challenges the tourist view of Scotland. Calder writes, "Americans and Germans will be challenged to set their romantic conceptions of Scotland against the frustrating reality of modern urban life" (219). That is, he argues, *Trainspotting* gives a "very nasty, very unheathery" (238) picture of Scotland. Yet the image that *Trainspotting* presents to the world is not the primary political component of the novel and film.

Calder notes that Welsh is hugely popular with two particular audiences: people under thirty and residents of Edinburgh. From this popularity, Calder argues, there will be lasting "political, social and ethical consequences" to the "phenomenon" of Welsh (238). Most importantly for my argument, these "consequences" are unknowable until they are produced, as Calder writes, in "an unimaginable future Scotland where Scottish identities, surviving, as I am sure they will, are constructed in ways which I cannot foresee, through language in its habitual state of flux and new songs transforming old ones" (238). Welsh's fiction is oriented toward the future, toward the creation of these new forms of identity.

Out of Welsh's writing emerges a Welshian subjectivity. In *Trainspotting* and his other fiction, Welsh details a new configuration of literary character, a novel subjectivity emerging from the contemporary urban Scotland where most of his work takes place. These novel subjectivities negotiate class and race politics, issues of national identity, and psychological conceptions of selfhood as they struggle to invent new ways of living in the contemporary world. At the same time, it is important to note that Welsh's subjectivities are not simply a representation of what it is like to be Scottish or to live in Scotland in the twenty-first century. Susan Hageman, in her introduction to *Studies in Scottish Fiction: 1945 to the Present,* writes that new Scottish fiction has little interest in defining "Scottish." Reacting against "market-oriented, totalized views of Scotland," Hageman argues that, in contemporary Scottish fiction, "national identity is dealt with obliquely, but honestly, in their texts; and it is precisely their lack of a magisterial vision of Scotland which makes them relevant to other 'small' literatures in English" (12–13). I take "small" here to be akin to what Deleuze and Guattari call "minor literature." A small, or minor, literature reworks a "major" language in order to produce new enunciations, to say things that cannot be said in the major language. Deleuze and Guattari write of Kafka, a Jew in Czechoslovakia, forging a minor literature within German. Welsh's use of Scots dialect within the major language of English, while by no means exactly the same as Kafka's use of German, carves out a space of expression for a novel form of identity.

Simon Frith, an English professor living in Scotland, writes, "Whenever I discuss Scottishness with Scottish students the consensus is that the only good indicator of a Scot is a Scottish accent" (3). If this is indeed the case, the aliens of "The Rosewell Incident" nicely illustrate the power of minor literature to create a new form of subjectivity, as they become Scottish through their ability to adopt a Scottish voice. Deleuze and Guattari call this power "the possibility to express another possible community and to forge the means for another consciousness and another sensibility" (*Kafka* 17). Welsh's use of Scottish does more than represent Scottish voices. Welsh shows readers that writing creates a novel form of subjectivity, a form of subjectivity that might bear close relation to the human but is not simply a subset of human invention. Literature does not merely reflect life; as Deleuze writes, "To write is certainly not to impose a form (of expression) on the matter of lived experience" ("Literature" 1). Literary characters are more than formal expressions of a writer's world. What Welsh creates in his writing is not only a reflection of the life of lower-class Scotland in the age of late capitalism. The realistic representations of his novels certainly have some political valence. Alan Freeman argues just such a point when he discusses the portrayal of "working class and underclass life" in *Trainspotting:* "Focusing on social margins not only affirms their inhabitants but also illuminates the centre against which they are defined and, in this novel, Welsh dramatises the repressive processes of post-industrial individualism" (251). Freeman locates the political efficacy of *Trainspotting* in its ability to articulate the repressive relation between marginalized and normative culture. *Trainspotting,* in focusing on the margins, implicitly critiques the powers that have enforced this marginalization. I want to argue that the political power of Welsh's fiction lies not just in these realistic representations but also in the creative potentials that the novels engender.

The expression of "another possible community" and the forging of "the means for another consciousness and another sensibility" are not means to a greater understanding among various peoples; it is not as if one can read a Welsh novel and then feel that he or she now understands what it is like to be a member of a certain Scottish class. A political reading of Welsh does not find its end in a movement from an understanding of his representations to a critique of the system that produced the lives being represented. Rather, his fiction details what Hardt and Negri in *Empire* call "the very unfolding of life itself" (30). In *Trainspotting* and his other works, Welsh creates a form of life that emerges into a "new" world of biopolitical power. Hardt and Negri write, "The great industrial and financial powers thus produce not only commodities but subjectivities. They produce agentic subjectivities within the biopolitical context: they produce needs, social relations, bodies, and minds—which is to say, they produce producers" (32). These subjectivities are not merely repressed individuals; in fact, Hardt and Negri argue that there is nothing inherently positive or negative about this production of subjectivity: "The constant functioning of social machines in their various apparatuses and assemblages produces the world along with the subjects and objects that constitute it" (28). The center cannot be critiqued from the margins. Welsh's novels are not critical of the world. They create a "minor literature" that closely details ways of living that are not mere critiques of the "major," or dominant, form of life. Rather, Welsh's minor use of English highlights the transformative possibilities that exist within "standard" English.

As the aliens of "The Rosewell Incident" adopt what Harry Ritchie calls "the noticeably lower-class nature of some of [new Scottish fiction's] most prominent subject-matter, language and authorial CVs" (3), the world needs to enlist "some of the CCS top boys, who had the confidence of the aliens, to help with the translation" (Welsh, "Rosewell" 215). In other words, to understand Welsh and his brethren, even the "English"-speaking world seems to need help. This idea that Welsh needs a translator is not merely a matter of concern within his fiction. Gerald Howard, an editor at Norton, the American publisher of *Trainspotting*, calls Welsh's "deployment of contemporary Scots demotic, a rich brew of industrial-strength profanity and slang" (348). Howard writes that "when we signed up Irvine Welsh's first novel, *Trainspotting*, I joked that it was going to be Norton's first foreign language publication" (348). But this claim that *Trainspotting* is written in a foreign language is more than a joke. Norton's American edition of *Trainspotting* comes with a glossary at the back of the book, directly following the last page of the novel. No glossary appears in its British editions, and the American edition gives no attribution for the glossary. This absence of commentary serves, along with the glossary, to help render the book foreign to American audiences, with its implicit claim that an American reader will need to access the glossary— presumably written by a translator fluent in Scots–American English translation—to fully understand the novel. This is not quite the case.

Prior to the publication of the novel's American edition, "A *Trainspotting* Glossary" was published in the *Paris Review*, accompanied by a note by Howard. Howard writes that, because of Welsh's language, "American readers might feel the need for linguistic training wheels" (348). Howard and his assistant wrote the glossary, or "doped out many of the definitions from context" (348), all of which was finally "vetted and completed by Irvine Welsh himself" (348). Keeping up the "joke," Howard writes that readers of the glossary can now "impress your friends with your correct usage of such terms as *radge, square go, biscuit-ersed*, and, of course, the all-purpose term of aggression and/or endearment, *cunt*" (348), which is defined as an "all-purpose term for someone else, either friendly or unfriendly" (346).

Those who adapted Welsh's novels as films have also worried about the ability of American ears to understand Welsh's Scottish accents. The film of *Trainspotting* redubbed the voice of one character before the film's American release, and the film of *The Acid House* was fitted with subtitles for its American release. Frank Begbie, the character whose voice was redubbed, says of two Canadian tourists he meets on a train in Edinburgh, who have trouble understanding his question, "Whair's it yis come fae then?" (Welsh, *Trainspotting* 114). "These foreign cunts've goat trouble wi the Queen's fuckin English, ken" (115). To get these foreigners to understand him, Begbie says, "Ye huv tae speak louder, slower, n likesay mair posh, fir the cunts to understand ye" (115). Begbie's speaking voice, as written by Welsh, obviously marks both national and class distinctions. He defines his dialect as "the Queen's fuckin English," and he cannot understand why people from another English-speaking country might have trouble understanding him. Likewise, Begbie's need to speak with a higher-class, "posh" accent points to a wide class divide between tourists with disposable income and working-class people like himself. While a glossary might well serve to make Begbie more comprehensible to an American or Canadian audience, it also serves to make him the "foreign cunt," the other. His language becomes nonstandard, something to translate, to understand through its relation to a normalized, standard, American or English English. Begbie's "Queen's fuckin English" becomes a subset of a broader English understandable by all English-speaking people.

Such attempts at translation ignore the inventive possibilities of minor literature. To understand Welsh's characters as simply speaking a bastardized version of a "proper" and understandable English that can be readily translated ignores the creative potential of this bastardization. That is, as Deleuze and Guattari write, "what can be said in one language cannot be said in another, and the totality of what can and can't be said varies necessarily with each language and with the connections between these languages" (*Kafka* 24). The connections between Welsh's Scots dialect and standard American and English English cannot be erased through glossary writing, dubbing and subtitling, or even through speaking "louder, slower, n likesay mair posh." Welsh's characters' usage of language is vital precisely because it "bring[s] to light new grammatical or syntactic powers" (Deleuze, "Preface" lv). That is, Welsh creates new possibilities of life within language. He articulates how novel subjectivities resist, and even refute, traditional notions of identity formation, psychology, and characterization as they begin to imagine ways of living in an "unimaginable, future Scotland." While not literally "alien" like the novel subjectivities of "The Rosewell Incident," Welsh's characters illustrate the widely varying forms of life that might live in this world. It is important to note that these novel subjectivities, even as they reconfigure the psychological, sociological, and political, are not necessarily critical representations. Freeman argues, "Unable to become an independent 'I,' a fully formed, stable self with the power of agency . . . each of Welsh's characters suffers the stasis of existence outside of social progression" (256). It is precisely this inability to become "an independent 'I,'" to become a subject, to be translated into understanding, that allows the creation of novel subjectivities. I want to argue that what Freeman calls the "stasis of existence" of Welsh's characters is actually a difficult search for silence that recurs throughout Welsh's fiction.

Welsh's fiction proliferates with characters that exemplify the difficulty of cultivating silence, from the junky of *Trainspotting* mentioned above to the narrator of *Marabou Stork Nightmares* who is in a coma but haunted by multilevel voices, to the narrator of *Filth* whose first-person narrative is constantly interrupted by the musings of a tapeworm in his gut, to the many characters in the short stories of *The Acid House* who seek silence through obsession, drugs, and suicide. As Welsh's characters seek silence, the outside world holds on. This desire for silence is nearly impossible to satisfy. The world persists.

As they crave silence, Welsh's characters continually fall into what Deleuze calls "a hole." In response to an interview question about his life, Deleuze speaks of "an eight year hole" after the writing of his first book, in which he "produced nothing." He remembers these years "only abstractly" ("Philosophy" 138), but rather than mourning these years as lost time, he locates this hole as an important space regarding the production of his subsequent work. Such holes, for Deleuze, are interesting not because they are sights of lost or repressed memories to be recovered, but because they are spaces of silence, becoming, and production:

> That's what I find interesting in people's lives, the holes, the gaps, sometimes dramatic, but sometimes not dramatic at all. There are catalepsies, or a kind of sleepwalking through a number of years, in most lives. Maybe it's in these holes that movement takes place. Because the real question is how to make a move, how to get through the wall, so you don't keep on banging your head against it. Maybe by not moving around too much, not talking too much, avoiding false moves, staying in places devoid of memory. (138)

Welsh's characters continually fall into such holes. Some—the narrators of *Marabou Stork Nightmares* and *Filth* especially—forget or even repress dramatic events, while others—most of the characters in *Trainspotting* and *The Acid House*—seem to have nothing to forget.

Regardless of motive, the desire for silence, the desire to fall into a hole, remains constant in Welsh's fiction. The persistence of this desire—rather than the secrets, failures, repressions, and social formations that are being forgotten—is the key component of a Welshian subjectivity. His characters resist, and even reconfigure, traditional narratives that read characters as psychological, social, or political representations. Something other than a critique of the current state of the world is at work as his characters oscillate between silence and the world. Welsh's writing continually produces new life forms, emergent subjectivities falling into and crawling out of holes in the world.

## *Trainspotting:* "Less tae life"

Two-thirds of the way through *Trainspotting,* Mark Renton, in the throes of heroin withdrawal, says, "Thir must be less tae life than this" (197), "this" being the physical pain and psychic hallucinations that accompany his withdrawal. By this point in the novel, a reader will have witnessed Renton in various stages of addiction and withdrawal. The novel's sections, connected to Renton's state of addiction, are chronologically titled "Kicking," "Relapsing," "Kicking Again," and "Blowing It," the section in which the above citation appears. The novel opens with Renton and his friend Sick Boy in need of a fix and ends with Renton thinking of himself as "a junky who has just ripped off his best mates" (343). In between, Renton and his fellow junkies continually move between two worlds. The first world, the world of "normal" society, is the world of "life," as described by Renton.

> Choose life. Choose mortgage payments; choose washing machines; choose cars; choose sitting on a couch watching mind-numbing and spirit-crushing game shows, stuffing fuckin junk food intae yir mooth. Choose rotting away, pishing and shiteing yersel in a home, a total fuckin embarrassment tae the selfish, fucked-up brats ye've produced. Choose life. (187)

For Renton, heroin addiction is "choos[ing] no tae choose life" (188). Addiction sloughs off the normative narrative of consumerist life for a world that is something less than life, the world of heroin addiction and silence. "Less" should not be taken as a moral or qualitative measurement, or even as a subversive maneuver. It is first and foremost simply a quantitative measurement. The life of addiction is a simplified kind of life, a reduction process of the concerns of everyday life. As Renton says,

> Whin yir oan junk, aw ye worry aboot is scorin. Oaf the gear, ye worry aboot loads ay things. Nae money, cannae git pished. Goat money, drinkin too much. Cannae git a burd, nae chance ay a ride. Git a burd, too much hassle, cannae breathe withoot her gitting oan yir case. Either that, or ye blow it, and feel aw guilty. Ye worry about bills, food, bailiffs, these Jambo Nazi scum beatin us, aw the things ye couldnae gie a fuck aboot whin yuv goat a real junk habit. Yuv just goat one thing tae worry aboot. The simplicity ay it aw. (133)

Addiction is simplification. The junky reduces his or her encounters with the world: cutting off friends, commodities, sex, family, sports, and so on, in favor of a single connection with heroin. Even the notion of choice undergoes a reduction process; the junky simply does what is required to get more junk. Renton shows how this reduction process works: "Ah love nothing (except junk), ah hate nothing (except forces that prevent me getting any) and ah fear nothing (except not scoring)" (21). Throughout *Trainspotting*, Renton and his friends continually fall into and emerge from the silencing hole of addiction. They constantly emerge from addiction reconfigured, somewhere else, not necessarily better or worse. Addiction and nonaddiction are the speed and slowness of life and something "less tae life."

Early in the novel, heroin addiction is described as a withdrawal from otherness. "The real junky . . . doesnae gie a fuck aboot anybody else" (7). "The fuckers dinnae exist fir us. Nae cunt does" (16). "The cunt was beginning no tae exist fir us" (6). People around the junky become encompassed by silence. During a binge, Renton thinks of a friend sitting right next to him: "It's the first words ah kin remember hearing um say for a few days. Obviously the cunt's spoken ower this period. He must huv, surely tae fuck" (51–52). Through a growing silence, Welsh's junkies move toward a state where "the outside world means fuck all tae us" (87). The approach to this space is not an inward movement away from the world and toward the self. Rather, this space is approached slowly, not through movement, but through an arrest of all motion. "It's a challenge tae move: but it shouldnae be. Ah can move. It has been done before. By definition, we, humans, likes, are matter in motion" (177). Heroin brings the junky close to a complete stop, where movement is only a memory: "It has been done before." The *Trainspotting* junky falls into an inhuman slowness, a slowness that distances the junky from both the outside world and any space of interior subjectivity.

At the same time, the desire to achieve this slowness is not a desire to transcend the self or the world, but just a temporary strategy. Speaking of the cycle of addiction, Renton says, "Ah jist intend tae keep right on to the end of the road" (188). The junky in *Trainspotting* continually oscillates between silence and the world, between "life" and "less tae life." As Renton thinks during one movement from silence to the world, "It was amazing, he decided, how things like sex and Hibs, which were nothing to him when he was on smack, suddenly became all-important" (150). Conversely, on heroin, he thinks, "At least with smack, there is no room for all the other crap" (132). As I note above, this oscillation structures the novel. This oscillation also structures the form of junky subjectivity that continually emerges from *Trainspotting*.

The *Trainspotting* junky is a matter of speed and slowness. Heroin addiction in *Trainspotting* is a slowing down of the engagement with both the self and the other, a pause, a falling into a hole. But this slowing down inevitably speeds up again and leads back to another encounter with otherness. Such oscillation becomes a way of life for Welsh's junkies. The persistence of this movement of constantly changing speed creates a continually emerging subject. This novel subject, the oscillating junky, can be difficult to say anything about. *Trainspotting* pays little attention to character motivation; Renton's continual cycling between the silent hole of addiction and an attachment to the world never gets attributed to any specific set of problems or concerns. Only a few pages are dedicated to decisions to stop or start heroin use. The movement from kicking to relapsing happens in a sentence or two. After two pages of detailed description of his "intense preparation" for getting off heroin, Renton oscillates back to it in a sentence: "Ah need the old 'slowburn,' a soft, come-down input" (16). Much later in the novel, after more oscillation, Renton decides that "Ah'm off tae Johnny Swan's for ONE hit, just ONE FUCKIN HIT tae get us ower this long, hard, day" (177). This "ONE hit" leads to an overdose, which leads to Renton's family forcing him to kick again, setting up further oscillations. Of course, physical addiction plays a part in Renton's continual relapsing. What is more interesting, though, is how *Trainspotting* downplays psychic motivations and undermines attempts to understand *why* Welsh's junkies continually crave the "wee bit ay silence" of addiction.

In a section of *Trainspotting* called "Searching for the Inner Man," Renton considers normative psychological narratives that might explain his behavior. He neither refutes nor accepts these explanations. He says, "Ah've been referred tae a variety of counsellors, wi backgrounds ranging fae pure psychiatry through clinical psychology to social work" (181). Renton sums up a psychiatrist's diagnosis:

> Ah have an unresolved relationship wi ma deid brother, Davie, as ah huv been unable tae work oot or express ma feelings about his catatonic life and subsequent death. Ah have oedipal feelings towards ma mother and an attendant unresolved jealously towards ma faither. Ma junk behavior is anal in concept, atten-tion-seeking, yes, but instead of withholding the faeces tae rebel against parental authority, ah'm pittin smack intae ma body tae claim power over it vis-à-vis society in general (184–185).

A drug counselor

> feels that ma concept ay success and failure only operates on an individual rather than an individual and societal level. Due tae this failure tae recognise societal reward, success (and failure) can only ever be fleeting experiences for me, as that experience cannae be sustained by the socially-supported condoning of wealth, power, status, etc., nor, in the case ay failure, by stigma or reproach (185–186).

I quote these two diagnoses at length to show that Renton does indeed think about the workings of his subjectivity. He says, "Ah've pondered ower a loat ay it, and ah'm willin tae explore it; ah don't feel defensive aboot any ay it" (185). At the same time, such narratives have little to nothing to do with Renton's

subjectivity. While he does not reject the truth of these diagnoses, he does not connect them to his life. "Fucked if ah could
see the connection between any ay that and me takin smack, but"
(184). He says, "Talking about it extensively has done fuck all
good" (185). Considering his drug counselor's diagnosis,
Renton says, "What Tom's trying tae say, ah suppose, is that ah
dinnae gie a fuck. Why?" (186). This "why" question cannot be
answered. Renton cannot explain why he does not "gie a fuck,"
and he cannot explain why he continually returns to heroin.
*Trainspotting* gives no reasons for drug addiction; instead, the
novel undermines this course of inquiry. Renton asks, "Why is it
that because ye use hard drugs every cunt feels that they have a
right tae dissect and analyse ye?" (187).

Engaging this question is important. Given the critical apparatus that I have employed throughout this work, I could easily
discuss Welsh as an "anti-oedipal" writer. Deleuze and
Guattari's configuration of the unconscious can offer a counter-
explanation that might allow one to understand Renton's
behavior. As he or she reduces the world, the junky moves
toward an inward disappearance, toward what Deleuze and
Guattari call a "Body without Organs" (BwO), or "what
remains when you take everything away. What you take away is
precisely the phantasy, and significances and subjectifications as
a whole" (*Thousand* 151). Achieving a BwO, in this case, is a
reduction process, a blotting out of meaning and encounters
with otherness. While the BwO can take on many forms, what
Deleuze and Guattari call "the drugged body" is most relevant
here. Deleuze and Guattari cite William S. Burroughs on just
such a body: "the drugged body: 'a junky . . . wants to be cool-
cooler-COLD. But he wants The Cold . . . INSIDE . . . so he
can sit around with a spine like a frozen hydraulic jack . . . his
metabolism approaching Absolute Zero'" (qtd. in *Thousand*
153–154). Welsh describes a strikingly similar situation in
*Trainspotting*. "It's cauld; very fuckin cauld . . . It's freezing,
but movement only makes ye caulder . . . the trick is tae be as
still as possible. It's easier than dragging yourself across the flair
tae switch that fuckin fire oan . . . It's really fuckin cauld man"
(95). The junky approaches absolute zero, a point where the
whole world becomes frozen, where everything stops; identity,
the self, others, and the whole world disappear in the space of "a
wee bit ay silence."

A reader can easily imagine Mark Renton responding to this description just as he responds to other discussions of his behavior: "Fucked if ah could see the connection between any ay that and me takin smack, but" (184). Saying that Renton has made himself a BwO is just as irrelevant here as saying that he has unresolved oedipal issues. Both descriptions cover over the singularity of Renton in favor of a more general term: oedipal subject, anti-oedipal subject. While the Deleuzian configuration seems more fitting here, it can be just as dangerous for the reader of Welsh if it simply serves to provide an explanation or understanding of Welsh's novel subjectivity. And in Welsh's *Marabou Stork Nightmares,* explanation and understanding become equated with acts of violence, further complicating questions of analysis and interpretation.

## *Marabou Stork Nightmares:* "This is what I have instead of a life"

While the characters in *Trainspotting* use heroin to move toward silence, Roy Strang, the narrator of *Marabou Stork Nightmares,* falls into a different kind of hole: a coma that results from a suicide attempt. Readers do not learn about this suicide attempt until much later in the book; such withholding of information points to the importance of secrets in Strang's narrative. Unlike *Trainspotting,* where character motivation has little underlying motive, Strang's suicide attempt and desire to stay in a coma are motivated by a secret that even he cannot remember. The novel's big secret—that Strang is primarily responsible for the kidnapping and gang rape of an acquaintance—does not get revealed until the last chapter. But *Marabou Stork Nightmares* is not only a novel about the guilt and retribution surrounding this brutal event.

A novel subjectivity emerges from the intersection of Strang's secret and his coma. His forgetting of the past motivates him to stay in the hole he has fallen into: "I do not wish to remember where I was before. I am averse to my past; it is an unsavoury blur which I have no wish to attempt to pull into focus" (*Marabou* 4). The silence he projects toward the outside world prevents any communication. When his doctors and his family try to reach him, he tries to cut off this encounter with otherness: "But they were trying to disturb me, trying to wake me; the way they always did. They willnae let this sleeping dog lie. They always interfere. When the cunts start this shite it makes things get aw distorted and I have to try to go deeper" (3). Even as he shows no outward reaction, the outside world does not give up. Strang continually withdraws "deeper" into his own head to flee the prodding of the world: "But they keep trying; even from in here I can feel them. Trying to stick another tube up my arse or something similar, something which constitutes a breach of my personal no no can't have this . . . change the subject, keep control" (7). But just as Renton learns in *Trainspotting,* Strang realizes that the world continually returns.

In his coma, Strang oscillates between three worlds: the present world of his hospital room; the past, as he remembers how events have led to his present "vegetative state"; and a metaphoric world, the "Marabou Stork Nightmares," in which he is in Africa hunting the Marabou Stork of the novel's title. He describes his attempt to keep these worlds separate, and the unavoidable encounters that populate his seemingly silent coma:

> Down here in the comforts of my vegetative state, inside my secret world I can fuck who I want, kill who I please, no no no nane ay that no no no I can I do the things I wanted to do, the things I tried to do, up there in the real world. No comeback. Anyway, *this* world's real enough to me and I'll stay down here out of the way, where they can't get to me, at least until I work it all out . . . It hasn't been so easy recently. Characters and events have been intruding into my mind, psychic gatecrashers breaking in on my private party. Imposing themselves . . . This is what I have instead of a life. (17)

These "psychic gatecrashers" are numerous, and Strang continually has difficulty hiding from them. As he attempts to "work it all out" in silence, his three worlds continually overlap. Familial visits continually pull him toward the "real world"; memories of the past intrude on his metaphoric "secret world"; thoughts on social issues such as Scottish nationhood and football violence constantly interrupt his narrative world. All of this overlap is portrayed on the page through various tricks of typography. Voices from the "real world"—family, friends, doctors, nurses—are presented in a smaller typeface than Strang's narrative, thoughts, and memories. Movement between worlds is signified by type that breaks with traditional line format. For instance, when a doctor shines a light into his eyes, Strang is wrested from his metaphoric world:

    up — — —
    coming
    — — — — — — — I'm. (5)

As he flees back toward the world in his head, he goes

    DEEPER
            DEEPER
                   DEEPER. (5)

As the novel progresses, readers learn that many components of Strang's metaphoric world have both "real world" and symbolic resonances. Much of his metaphorics could be read as his "work[ing] it all out" on an unconscious level in preparation for a conscious expression of his "secret." In other words, on a certain level, his metaphoric world calls out for psychological interpretation. As Strang says to Sandy Jamieson, his partner in the metaphoric hunt for the Marabou Stork, "You're a metaphor, Jamieson. You don't exist outside of me. I can't be angry with nothing, you're just a manifestation of my guilt" (6). But more is at work.

Strang loses control of his symbols throughout his narrative. His metaphors take on a life of their own, continually slipping from his control. The psychological narrative that Strang is working out in his coma—briefly, that his dysfunctional family, particularly years of sexual abuse at the hands of his uncle, led to his violent attack on the woman he rapes—is continually interrupted as he oscillates between worlds. He gets angry at his metaphors; memories of the past and events of the present invade his story. Even as he creates it, he resists the familial narrative. As he moves from memories to the present of his hospital room, he flees the "ugly world" inhabited by his parents: "MUMMY DADDY, NICE TO SEE YOU IS IT FUCK . . . DON'T WANT TO GET CLOSER TO YOUR UGLY WORLD GOT TO GO DEEPER, DEEPER DOWN, GOT TO HUNT THE STORK, TO GET CONTROL" (11). The "ugly world" that contains Strang's "dirty little secret" cannot serve as full explanation for the events of his life. His secrets—both his history of abuse and the rape of his acquaintance—and his coma keep him oscillating among three worlds. This constant oscillation is precisely what he has "instead of a life." At the intersection of past, present and metaphor, a novel subjectivity emerges. Strang, comatose and full of secrets, moves toward a future that will elude what he sees as the logical end of his narrative: "to wake up, to take my place in society and all that shite" (10). Like Renton, who flees the "life" that Strang succinctly defines here, Strang cannot simply "wake up" into life. The singularity of his experience, what he has "instead of a life" is a subjectivity regulated by a coma state that resists and reconfigures all attempts at interpretation, understanding, and "working out."

Strang's comatose body alters his experience of time. Fluctuating between worlds, Strang knows that he is experiencing time differently. Considering a past event, he thinks, "As my memory is practically non-existent, this could have been a few days ago or since the beginning of time" (4). The coma breaks up the seeming forward movement of time—from past, through present, to future—that would allow him to work out his past in the present so that he could emerge into a healthy future self. The coma is a sort of pause, a suspension of time. Richard Doyle, in *Wetwares: Experiments in Postvital Living*, writes that the comatose body dissolves "the opposition between 'past' and 'future'" (157). In the present, in what Strang calls "the real world," the comatose body is silent, without response. His family, his doctors, and nurses continually try to pull him out of his suspended state, out of the past and into the present: "ALWAYS FUCKIN HERE. ALWAYS ASSUMING I WANT THEIR FUCKIN PRESENCE" (*Marabou* 10). But their presence, their present, is precisely what Strang does not want. In such a world, his future is already determined as his "tak[ing] my place in society, and all that shite." "Working out" the past and resolving his secrets (he has already been legally acquitted of the rape) will throw him into life, into the present world of his familial drama. The work of the coma prevents this linear narrative from occurring.

In his coma, Strang cannot choose how he will reenter the "real world." His coma is an interruption, a fold of subjectivity that resists linear time, resists resolution and understanding. Having fallen into a hole of silence, he cannot determine where he will emerge. Doyle writes that the coma's pause reconfigures the way that the comatose body will encounter the future: "Such a logic of interruption—to encounter the future, let it break you up, put you in a coma, kill you—cannot . . . be chosen" (153). The coma's "logic of interruption" resonates strongly with Deleuze's concept of falling into a hole. Movement takes place in such holes, but such movement cannot be controlled, whether by a psychological narrative or by the logic of a self in control. Strang loses control, his story is continually interrupted; he cannot steer his narrative toward a resolution that will place him back in the present, in full presence. He cannot force his metaphoric world and his narrative of the past to serve the present as agents of a working out of the past. Doyle writes, "As with exotic derivatives—those morphologies of capital whose encounter with the future depends crucially on an interval of non-knowledge, a dead zone of value—the comatose body is constituted by its noisy, inarticulable silence" (159). Such "non-knowledge" differs immensely from the logic of secrets. The "non-knowledge" of a coma leads not toward a predictable resolution but toward an unpredictable future. The coma's interruption cannot be interpreted away, whether in a movement from symbolic to real, from unconscious to conscious, or from "instead of a life" to life.

The comatose body exists at the intersection of conscious and unconscious. As Strang withdraws from the "real" world, he thinks, "This means I'm back to where they can't get to me: deep in the realms of my own consciousness" (*Marabou* 7). Doyle describes the comatose body as "literally an unconscious, alive" (157), which is an apt description of Strang. Doyle continues, "Comatose bodies become conscious subjects through the continually, hopefully, expected interruption called the future" (167). As Strang continually moves toward and resists the interruption of the future, his (un)consciousness continually reconfigures the function of the secret, so that it ceases to be about his family and his past.

Strang's coma wrests the secret from its usual function as something to be disclosed, revealed, or discovered. The logic of interruption that organizes Strang's multiple stories prevents the "coming to terms with the past" narrative from dominating. *Marabou Stork Nightmares* does more than move in a straight line from denial to acceptance, from the past to the future, and, as the reader finds out, from guilt to retribution. Along with the coma, the secret structures Strang's oscillation between worlds. Deleuze and Guattari write of this structuring function: "The more the secret is made into a structuring, organizing form, the thinner and more ubiquitous it becomes, the more its content becomes molecular, at the same time as its form dissolves" (*Thousand* 289). The secret is everywhere and nowhere. Strang realizes this when he considers the symbolic import of the Marabou Stork: "I want to keep hunting the Stork. The Stork's the personification of all this badness. If I kill the Stork I'll kill the badness in me" (*Marabou* 9). Strang knows that he has something hidden, some dark secret. Killing the stork stands for resolving the secret. And, as I quote above, when the secret is dealt with, when the stork is killed, "then I'll be ready to come out of here, to wake up, to take my place in society and all that shite" (9–10). But the "hunt," the quest for understanding and interpretation, continually gets interrupted. The secret refuses to function as something to be uncovered; it resists the binary of secret/disclosure.

Deleuze and Guattari write that the secret serves little function as part of a binary. Trying to figure out a secret, "drawing up a list of these reasons (shame, treasure, divinity, etc.) has limited value as long as the secret is opposed to its discovery as in a binary machine having only two terms, the secret and disclosure, the secret and desecration" (*Thousand* 286). The secret is not one term in a binary. It is a movement, or as Deleuze and Guattari write, a collective assemblage: "Every secret is a collective assemblage. The secret is not at all an immobilized or static notion" (287). It is precisely for this reason that Strang forgets his need to discover his secret. Instead, the secret and the coma together produce the future, the ethical encounter with otherness that has little to do with resolution and the ability to live in the "real world."

After enunciating his need to hunt the stork, to search out his secret, Strang forgets his interpretive quest and becomes a pragmatist. While still somewhat resistant, he begins to give in to the logic of interruption, not trying to figure out where things come from and not trying to sort out, to understand, or to interpret. "All I have is the data I get. I don't care whether it's produced by my senses or my memory or my imagination. Where it comes from is less important than the fact that it *is*. The only reality is the images and texts" (*Marabou* 16). As the novel progresses, Strang moves more easily between the three worlds, and readers can easily start to make connections between Strang's three worlds. For instance, Strang remembers living in South Africa and having his dad point out a Marabou Stork, which leads him to further remember, "That night I had my first Marabou Stork nightmare" (74). As the novel moves toward its conclusion, the resonances increase as the borders between the three worlds decrease. Strang reveals his secrets: his abuse at the hands of his uncle, his role in the rape, and his attempted suicide. The puzzle seems to be solved; readers can fit all the pieces together and diagnose Roy Strang.

We learn that Strang's memories were repressed because he could not come to terms with his active role in the rape; we learn that, instead of being nicknamed "Dumbo Strang" for the big ears he remembers himself having, he was called "Captain Beaky" for "my spindly legs, my large overcoat, my massive beak . . . I have no visible ears, I never really had much in the way of ears, it was always my nose, Captain Beaky, they used to call me at the school . . . it wasn't the ears, my memory hasn't been so good" (264, ellipses in the original). We learn that Sandy Jamieson is "Jimmy Sandison," a football player who was on TV when Strang attempted suicide. A reader can easily interpret Strang's narrative world as an expression of his desire to die because he cannot face the guilt of what he did. As he remembers his suicide attempt, Strang thinks, "This was about the only resolution that made sense. Death was the way forward" (255). But not in the way that he thought.

After a "blissful void" (256) following his suicide attempt, Strang "woke up lying in a tropical grassland, with Jamieson mopping my sweating brow" (256). That is, the suicide attempt produced the coma state and Strang's narrative world. In the end, Strang is pulled from this interpretative world in an unexpected way. The woman he raped returns and pulls Strang from his coma by "snipping my eyelids neatly off," and then she says, "I'm going to let you feel this, Roy! They say a man can hardly feel it, hardly feel the removal of his prick" (262) and "Let you taste it, like I had to" (263). "This is going in your mouth, Roy" (263). Strang is wrenched from his interpretive world and forced to encounter not a symbol of his guilt, but an actual person. "She's looking into my eyes, my lidless eyes and we see each other now . . . I understand her hurt, her pain, how it all just has to come out . . . We both understand everything" (263–264). Communication takes place through this act of retribution, and "understanding" occurs only through violence. Welsh's *Filth* escalates this violence, most of which is seen through the eyes of Bruce Robertson, the novel's narrator, who like Strang is another unconscious alive, full of secrets but resistant to interpretation.

## *Filth:* "Part of me is elsewhere"

Like *Marabou Stork Nightmares, Filth* is told from the perspective of a first-person narrator existing at the intersection of three voices. *Filth* is the first-person narration of racist, violent, and misogynist Scottish cop Bruce Robertson. Two voices, which the reader eventually learns are aspects of Robertson's unconscious, constantly interrupt Robertson's narrative. The first interruptive voice is that of "Carole," Robertson's estranged wife. This narrative appears printed in boldface, with "Carole" appearing in chapter headings. Eventually, readers learn Robertson's first secret through this voice: "Carole" expresses Robertson's thoughts, as he prowls the town—and commits a murder—dressed in his wife's clothes. The second interruptive voice is that of a tapeworm living in Robertson's gut. The worm's narrative interrupts Robertson's on the page, as text framed by the shape of the worm is written over, obliterating Robertson's narrative. As the worm grows, it dubs itself "Self" and eventually becomes the voice of Robertson's unconscious, letting the reader in on Robertson's other dark secrets: that his father is a rapist, a madman locked in prison, and that his stepfather constantly abused him as a child. As in *Marabou Stork Nightmares,* these three narrative threads eventually come together as the narrator is dying.

While these similarities are striking, it is also important to note that *Filth* is the first novel in which Welsh does not focus on the lower-class, drug-taking denizens of Edinburgh. To illustrate the distance between the subjects of Welsh's earlier work and the subject of *Filth,* Robertson comments on a "bohemian" poet he meets in a pub: "A jakey mumbling fuckin crap poems at people who dinnae want tae fuckin well hear them. So that's what they call art now, is it? Or some fuckin schemie writing aboot aw the fuckin drugs him n his wideo mates have taken" (Welsh, *Filth* 37). Even as Robertson differs in social situation from Welsh's other narrators, he shares at least two qualities with the other, novel Welshian subjects—Mark Renton and Roy

Strang—whom I have considered so far: a desire for some kind of silence, and a resistance to analysis.

Robertson does not fall into a silent hole in the ways—heroin addiction, coma—Renton and Strang do. Robertson's strategy involves an attempt to find silence by overwhelming the voices in his head with as much noise as possible. He realizes just how populated his unconscious is, so he tries to make it even more crowded, to get lost in the silence of total noise: "Get as many voices in your head as you can and hide in the crowd. We've got loads of them. Probably as many as there are worms eating away inside us" (234). Robertson tries to keep in constant motion as he tries to outrun his thoughts. "The problem with my game is that we're not great thinkers. We do. You have to keep doing, to find things to do" (73). Robertson uses work, sex, and television to keep a constant stream of voices screaming from the outside. Unable to sleep at night, he works constant overtime. When his overtime hours are cut, he turns to sex. "These cunts are trying tae kill us with this OT cutback because they know we cannae kip during the fuckin night, never could. They know we need very little sleep and that all we do in darkness is think and think and think. In order to stop thinking we have to fuck and then you get complications; financial in the case of hoors, social in the case of slags" (254). Still, the voices persist, and he grows more and more horrified of the night as the novel progresses: "No way will I sleep" (272), and "Too many anxiety attacks at night. I wish it was daylight for twenty-four hours" (274). He constantly plays music loudly and always has the television on. "More television. No. The channels, the voices, always the fuckin voices" (378). "I'm hearing the voices and I'm pressing the buttons on the handset to change channels but it's the voice in my head. That same, insistent soft voice, eating me up from the inside" (381). While he tries to silence this "insistent soft voice," he completely rejects the idea of examining the thoughts in his head.

Robertson sees his visits to prostitutes as a means of self-analysis. With a prostitute, he thinks, "This is therapy in its purest and simplest form . . . and the lesson today is: BRUCE ROBERT-SON" (223). Any attempts at analysis are met with fierce resistance. A coworker attempts to discuss his psychological state, and Robertson screams in his head, "GET ON WITH YOUR FUCKIN JOB AND STOP PLAYING THE AMATEUR PSY-CHOLOGIST" (340). His doctor, Rossi, asks him about what might be causing "a persistent nervous condition" (243), and Robertson replies that there is "nothing on my mind at all" (243). While Robertson is saying this, he inwardly seethes at Rossi, a general practitioner treating Robertson for tapeworms, thinking that "Rossi evidently wants to be a psychologist" and that he should just "dae yir fuckin job ya cunt" (243). As it turns out, the tapeworm, along with "Carole," provides the details for a psychological diagnosis of Robertson. At the same time, the sheer overdetermined nature of this diagnostic possibility calls any analysis into question.

As the tapeworm grows and covers over more and more of Robertson's text, it gathers more information about its "Host." This gathering of information is motivated by the worm's boredom: "There is not that much to do around here . . . Mine Host . . . You must be leading a far more interesting life than myself" (139). Out of this boredom, the worm decides that "I will sift through the food the Host ingests, probe the cells of the skin that I'm so attached to, assimilate all the bonnie data from the braw yin's consumption patterns and physical condition. To do this means I need to eat and eat and eat" (139). As the tapeworm, or "the Self" (108), as it begins to think of itself, continues to eat, it provides insight into Robertson's character. "The Self" says to him, "I can feel all your ghosts. You've internalised them Bruce" (242). The tapeworm reveals Robertson's childhood and adolescent traumas: being forced to eat coal (315); the favoritism given to his younger brother (316); his accidental murder of his brother (354), which leads to his stepfather exclaiming, "You're no ma son! You've never been ma fuckin son! You're filth!" (355). "The Self" reveals the secret of Robertson's father. As "the Self" narrates, Robertson's mother "was putting flowers on the grave of her dead brother" (381) when she

> was attacked by a man. She was beaten and raped. Molly gave a description and the man was apprehended. He was tried and convicted of a number of rapes and sexual assaults on women and men. It was revealed at his trial that this man suffered from mental problems: acute schizophrenia, depression, anxiety attacks. (381)

Bruce is the child of this rape. To compound this trauma, "the Self" also tells the story of Bruce's first girlfriend, Rhona. As the tapeworm tells it, Rhona wore a "metallic, leathery caliper" (369), and the couple was referred to by other adolescents as "The Son of the Beast and The Spastic" (372). To avoid such taunts, Robertson and Rhona one day take a shortcut through a golf course. A thunderstorm starts, and

> then there is a rumble in the sky and the rain comes teeming down. Then you see a large flash, followed by another rumble. Then you hear Rhona let out a strange yelp . . . and you turn around to see her briefly shrouded in an electrical glow as she is struck by a bolt of lightning. (373)

The tapeworm also understands how Robertson tries to "deal with" this trauma: "You need the job; hating, yet at the same time thriving on, its petty concerns. These concerns are enough to distract you from the Self you must only face up to at night between the extinguishing of the television set and the onset of a jittery and fitful descent into a physically bruising sleep" (260). Likewise, "Carole" understands that **The problem with Bruce is that he keeps it all in** (42). She also says, in an ironically reflective moment, **"Repressed people; you have to pity them more than anything else"** (122).

How can readers react to this? With direct access to all three narratives, readers are able to form connections that Robertson only makes, and resists, as he is dying. Near the end, Robertson reacts to the tapeworm's narrative by saying, "That is not true" (355). As "the Self's" voice persists, Robertson tries to distract himself with television, but fails. Likewise, he resists "Carole's" narrative. He acknowledges himself as Carole only because of a violent act, a kidnapping by thugs who recognize him as a cop. As they beat him up, he remembers "how this all started: that when Carole first left . . . we started wearing her clothes and it was like she was still with us but no really" (343). Violence is what brings these voices together, just as in *Marabou Stork Nightmares.*

This violence haunts any attempt on the reader's part to synthesize Robertson's three voices into one "Self." Such a bringing together is all too complete; synthesizing the three voices brings about a completeness akin to death. Robertson, of course, never attempts to bring all three voices together as one. He strongly resists any narrative that is centered on a human self. He belittles a coworker who is looking at him "in a deep, soulful and human way" (189) after Robertson had tried to save a man who was dying of a heart attack. More strongly, Robertson continually repeats the phrase "How did it make you feel?" (141, 173, 220, 343) in an ironic manner, parodying the human caring and communication that this question can imply. Furthering his resistance to any form of analysis, Robertson continually says such things as "You don't fuck about with Bruce Robertson. Same rules apply" (232). These "rules" are his strong resistance to any examination of psychological state or motivation that might force him to hear the voices in his head. He staunchly refuses to become a complete self.

Further, considering Robertson's three voices as part of one complete self leads to a far too obvious diagnosis. The sheer number of motivations provided for his behavior renders any analysis a parody. The diagnosis of his biological father's "mental problems: acute schizophrenia, depression, anxiety attacks" (381) mirror Bruce's behavior too perfectly. Likewise, the social traumas that Robertson suffered—abusive stepfather, girlfriend struck dead by lightning—fit together too neatly to serve as serious "explanations" for his behavior. Rather than bringing these three narratives together to point to the creation of a conflicted self, one might instead ask how the three voices function in the novel subjectivity of Bruce Robertson.

Robertson's resistance, his "rules," is exemplified by his pure resentment of the world. As he prepares for his suicide, he calls Carole to "talk. Sort out the divorce" (391). In anticipation of her arrival he puts on a T-shirt that says "YOU CAUSED THIS" (392), and prepares to hang himself from "the rafters of the attic . . . ready to drop out of the hatch as soon as she turns the key in the lock and pushes the door open. We'll land right in front of her in the hallway, so she'll have that on her conscience for the rest of her fucking life the fuckin whore and liar" (392). Robertson's actions here bear a striking similarity to Deleuze's description of Nietzsche's man of *ressentiment*:

> The man of *ressentiment* in himself is a being full of pain: the sclerosis or hardening of his consciousness, the rapidity with which every excitation sets and freezes within him, the weight of the traces that invade him are so many cruel sufferings. And, more deeply, *the memory of traces is full of hatred in itself and by itself.* It

is venomous and depreciative because it blames the object in order to compensate for its own inability to escape from the traces of the corresponding excitation. This is why *ressentiment's* revenge, even when it is realized, remains "spiritual," imaginary and symbolic in principle. (*Nietzsche* 116)

Robertson characterizes his suicide as a largely symbolic action, meant to place guilt on Carole's conscience. This final act of resentment is only the last in a series of encounters for Robertson. His every interaction with others is ruled by resentment. As he sums up his philosophy, "Every cunt has their Achilles' heel, and I always make a point of remembering my associates' ones. Something that crushes their self-image to a pulp. Yes, it's all stored for future reference" (20). Robertson's memory only functions as a repository for a future encounter designed to obliterate otherness. Deleuze writes that "Nietzsche himself presents memory as an unfinished digestion and the type of *ressentiment* as an anal type. This intestinal and venomous memory is what Nietzsche calls the spider, the tarantula, the spirit of revenge." (*Nietzsche* 116). Or the tapeworm. As the tapeworm says to Robertson as it re-presents his memories, "The urge to hurt, demean and control is great in you. To somehow get back at them" (389). The tapeworm knows that Robertson's unconscious, embodied in "the Self" of the tapeworm, endlessly enacts this "spirit of revenge" that "rules" Robertson's every encounter with otherness.

Early in the novel, "Carole" says, **"Part of me is elsewhere"** (2). As Robertson dies at the end of the novel, the tapeworm says, "I am gone, gone with the Host, leaving the screaming others, always the others, to pick up the pieces" (393). Bruce Robertson's dispersed subjectivity emerges between these two poles as a man of *ressentiment*. At the same time, as I argue in my discussion of Mark Renton, the singularity of Welsh's novel subjectivities cannot be covered over by more general terms. While resentment seems to drive Robertson's final action, it does not serve as a means of understanding his character.

* * *

Mark Renton, Roy Strang, and Bruce Robertson all share a desire to silence the world; in addition to this, they all strongly resist analysis and interpretation. Readers can react to these two things in infinite ways, ascribing Freudian denial, Deleuzian body without organ building, Nietzschean *ressentiment,* or myriad other interpretive tools to these characters. Any of these analyses might be valid, and certain interpretive tools would certainly prove more fruitful than others. But for a reader, or a literary critic, to encounter these subjects as *Welshian,* such interpretations must be forgotten. To engage the singularity of a Welshian novel subjectivity entails close consideration of the following questions: What are the components of this subject's literary existence? How do these characters gain material existence in the encounter between reader and writer?

## "Delirium," Literature, History, and Politics

As I have been arguing throughout this chapter, Welsh creates a world populated by "silence junkies" who strongly resist analysis. Both of these characteristics—desire for silence and resistance to analysis—point to a consciousness that is not centered on a fully realized, autonomous self. This is witnessed in *Trainspotting* as the junky's addiction to heroin (and the nonjunky's addiction to "life"), and in *Marabou Stork Nightmares* and *Filth* as the multiple voices inside the respective narrators' heads. In a sense, the citations I use at the head of my discussion of each novel point to a life not centered on a self. Renton's "less tae life" can be considered as an autonomous, stable self subtracted from "life"; what Strang has "instead of a life" is a life populated by multiple voices that a single self cannot keep control of; Robertson's "part of me is elsewhere" is a resentful admittance that Bruce Robertson is much more populated than the centered individual that he wishes to be. Renton's inability even to be interested in the question of why he continually oscillates between heroin addiction and "life" shows that he has no interest in finding his "self." Likewise, *Trainspotting* never provides glimpses into the psychic motivations and the inner lives of its characters. This is not a failing of the novel. Renton (and to a greater and lesser degree the other characters in *Trainspotting*) has no need for psychic motivations or inner life; such things are simply not part of his world. *Marabou Stork Nightmares* and *Filth* could not be further from *Trainspotting* in their supply of psychic, social, and even genetic motivations for their characters' behaviors. At the same time, none of these motivations can be strongly attached to Strang's and Robertson's selves. No center exists for the voices in their heads; no voice rules the others.

In the holes that they have fallen into, Strang and Robertson do not have any memory of, or access to, a self that might organize or control the various voices in their heads. For both, a self only emerges at the end of each novel, through violent acts of murder and suicide. In both cases, a self is arrived at only through death. I will consider the relation between violence, otherness, and ethics at the end of this chapter, but for now I want to consider the bulk of *Marabou Stork Nightmares* and *Filth,* wherein no self organizes the emergent subjectivities of Strang and Robertson. Neither narrator possesses the ability to control narrative, to produce meaning. As I note above, Strang loses control of his metaphors; he cannot "keep control" of the populations of the various worlds of his "vegetative state." Likewise, Robertson continually hears voices that he cannot control: "We hear voices . . . Aw the time. Do you ever hear them? All our life we've heard them. The worms" (*Filth* 333). In these characters, Welsh does not presuppose a human self; instead of a self, Welsh's characters consist of a metaphor, a coma state, a cross dresser, and a worm.

Robertson's doctor is speaking of worms, but he could just as easily be talking of selves in Welsh's fiction when he says, "They are harmless parasites, but they can be hard to get rid of" (131). Perhaps this is why such a strong antipsychological strain runs through Welsh's fiction, from Renton's complete indifference to all forms of psychology in the "Searching for the Inner Man" section of *Trainspotting* to Robertson's vehement "GET ON WITH YOUR FUCKIN JOB AND STOP PLAYING THE AMATEUR PSYCHOLOGIST" (340). In particular, Welsh's characters resist psychological narratives that are centered on the family as too simple explanations for the workings of the unconscious. Renton's response, "Radge, eh?" (*Trainspotting* 185) to the diagnosis of his "oedipal feelings towards ma mother and an attendant unresolved jealousy towards ma faither" (185) nicely typifies the novel's attitudes toward familial psychological narratives. Likewise, Robertson sarcastically says of his own violent behavior, "It was Daddy. I blame him. He was a bad man" (*Filth* 97). And Strang, of course, views his family as a nuisance that continually brings him to the present of his hospital room: "MUMMY DADDY, NICE TO SEE YOU IS IT FUCK . . . DON'T WANT TO GET CLOSER TO YOUR UGLY WORLD" (*Marabou* 11).

Evidence of this antipsychology also runs through Welsh's short fiction. There is the yuppie father in "The Acid House," who is eager to discuss his "terrible jealousy" toward his son with his men's group, so that he can "talk it through with other men who were in touch in with their feelings. The thought of having a genuine hang-up to share with the rest of the group thrilled him" (*Acid* 164). There is the final line "A Good Son," part of "The Sexual Disaster Quartet," in *The Acid House*. After sleeping with his mother, the son "passed his father on his way out of the room, he heard the old man say: Aye Oedipus, yir a complex fucker right enough" (*Acid* 61). In short, Welsh's fictional world cannot be explained or understood through a narrative that presupposes selves or family interactions as base explanations for the functions of either a conscious or an unconscious mind.

The resistance to analysis that runs through Welsh's characters is not something to be overcome by readers seeking a reflection of the world in the inner lives of Renton, Strang, and Robertson. Rather, these characters provide a way of rethinking traditional notions of selfhood and its place in the world. Deleuze argues that the ability to create this kind of rethinking is one of literature's most powerful, and delirious, aspects. He writes, "Literature is delirium, but delirium is not a father-mother affair: there is no delirium that does not pass through peoples, races, and tribes, and that does not haunt universal history" ("Literature" 4). In this formulation, literature becomes much more than a means for understanding the relation between the individual and the social. Literature leaves behind psychology as its novel subjectivities forge new connections with history and politics. Deleuze's "pass[ing] through" can be taken as a purposefully vague definition of these connections. That is, as the literary passes through the historical and the political, unforeseen configurations emerge, just as novel subjectivities emerge from heroin passing through Renton's body and from a tapeworm passing through Robertson's gut. All of these "passings through" are political, in that they all configure new ways of living in the world. It is because of this creative potential, this creation of new ways of life, that Deleuze and Guattari say of minor literatures, "Everything in them is political" (*Kafka* 17). Minor literature is political precisely because of its creativity, its always reconfigured way of linking the individual and the political. Minor literature is more interested in producing the future than it is in critiquing the present.

Deleuze and Guattari are not alone in noting that literature can have transformative political power. In *Marxism and Literature*, Raymond Williams argues that "creative practice" becomes political when it becomes interested in producing new ways of life. His conception of literature as a struggle resonates with Deleuze's delirium. Williams writes that when literature "becomes struggle—the active struggle for new consciousness through new relationships that is the ineradicable emphasis of the Marxist sense of self-creation—it can take many forms" (212). Williams sees new ways of life emerging from the production of new connections between individuals and society. Like Deleuze, and like me, Williams notes that this production of a new consciousness is unpredictable, tenuous, and oriented toward the future. He writes that this creative practice "is always difficult and often uneven . . . .For creativity and social self-creation are both known and unknown events, and it is still from grasping the known that the unknown—the next step, the next work—is conceived" (212). Fiction's creative potential is also its political potential. A one-to-one relation between the world of fiction and the world of politics cannot be articulated, because this relation only becomes apparent in the movement from the known to the unknown, in the passing through the present to the future.

Moving with Welsh's characters between the known and the unknown requires a silencing of both psychological selfhood and what de Man calls "critical acts of interpretation." He writes of Blanchot, in a critique that could easily be leveled at Welsh:

> Blanchot's criticism, starting out as an ontological meditation, leads back into the question of the temporal self. For him, as for Heidegger, Being is disclosed in the act of its self-hiding and, as conscious subjects, we are necessarily caught up in this movement of dissolution and forgetting. A critical act of interpretation enables us to see how poetic language always reproduces this negative movement, though it is often not aware of it. (*Blindness* 76)

Welsh' silence junkies show that falling into a hole of silence is not a "negative movement" that ground subjectivity in lack, but is instead a movement of becoming that produces singularities. One can easily uncover "negative movements" in Blanchot and Welsh. To do so is to miss the productive quality of movement in both writers. To read in order to uncover blind spots is to miss the movement that is produced through what Blanchot calls "tone" and Deleuze calls "style." "A critical act of interpretation" ignores that writers "bring to light new grammatical or syntactic powers" (Deleuze, "Preface" lv) that create new possibilities of life. Deleuze writes, "Syntactic creation or style—that is the becoming of language" ("Literature" 5). Through this becoming, subjectivities emerge. What comes out into Blanchot's "daylight" is such novel subjectivities: Renton, Strang, and Robertson. These subjectivities, like Blanchot's writer, need to silence "I," to cut themselves off from the world, to cut off the past, to cut off identity. Such a movement could be seen as a refutation of otherness, a solipsistic return to the self. But it is precisely this silencing, this pause before otherness, that produces subjects in Welsh's world.

An ethical response to Welsh's novel might work in a style that pays close attention to the emergence of a Welshian style of writing and of subjectivity, not in the style of a de Manian reading that notes blindnesses and the incompleteness of self. Welsh details an emergent form of subjectivity, a new configuration of literary subjectivity, springing forth both from his work and from his contemporary urban Scotland. He is not just representing Scotland; he is interrogating subjectivity and otherness, and reconfiguring the self. In cultivating silence, Welsh's characters negotiate class and race politics, issues of national identity, and psychological conceptions of selfhood; they illustrate the ethical imperative, for the contemporary literary critic, among others, to take such categories as neither givens nor constructs, but as movements always in a state of becoming, continually falling into and emerging from holes of silence.

If both Scottish fiction and Scottish politics are in the process of moving from the known to the unknown, both the connections between the two and the end products of these connections remain to be determined. That there is a connection between the future of Scottish literature and politics does not seem to be in doubt. Hageman writes, "Scotland, and especially urban culture, appears to have been reinvented recently, a process which has gone hand in hand with formal innovation" (12). The formal innovation of Welsh and other "new" Scottish writers creates strategies for living in the world. Perhaps this is why Frith writes that "in wondering what it means to be Scottish, I read novels not newspapers" (6). Novels have the power to create new linkages among individual, social, and political concerns. Frith writes that Scottish fiction reconfigures life precisely in its articulation of "a world shaped not only by English history and English culture . . . but also by Hollywood films and American television, by country music, jazz and rock, by cartoons, comics and video games . . . by European design and literature, by science and international academia" (6). Welsh's novel subjectivities emerge from this world at the same time as they continually produce ways of living in it. Rather than "grieve for selves that cannot be" (Freeman 260), *Trainspotting, Marabou Stork Nightmares,* and *Filth* actively produce subjectivities that can inhabit the future.

Welsh's characters, and his novels, have tenuous and fluctuating connections with contemporary Scotland; they exist at an intersection of family, nationalism, violence, misogyny, and drugs. His fiction resists outright critique; Welsh should not be read as providing case studies that point toward what has gone wrong with the world. At the same time the opposite tack should not be taken; Welsh's fiction is by no means utopian. The point is that it is impossible to say exactly how fiction and politics pass through each other. Andrew Ross, in his consideration of Edinburgh's William Wallace monument, shows that this passing through always leads in multiple directions.

Discussing the recent remodeling of the monument, what he calls "the makeover required of postmodern tourism" (100–101), Ross notes that a new statue of Wallace in the parking lot looks so much like Mel Gibson, the portrayer of Wallace in the film *Braveheart,* that it is often referred to as "the 'Mel Gibson statue'" (101). In addition to this concrete effect on historical representation, Ross notes that "*Braveheart* has drawn many competing claims on its symbolism" (101). "Not a few of the monument's daily American visitors hail from the South, where *Braveheart* has been adopted by the neo-Confederate movement as a potent political token of both Scottish and Confederate secession, and where its depiction of 'angry white males' has fed into recent attempts to celebrate cracker and redneck pride" (101). In addition, Ross uses his analysis of the

Wallace monument and *Braveheart* to point to the myriad directions Scotland's new political situation might lead to:

> Scotland's way forward may yet learn how to fuse a cosmopolitan tradition . . . with a tradition of popular sovereignty . . . Of course, Scottish experience also portends other, much less savory, futures; a one-way nativist path to parochial sclerosis, or the semi-periphery track of a "Celtic tiger" whose soul has been traded to the multinational leviathans of capital. Place your bets and stay tuned to Radio Caledonia! (107)

In other words, the future of Scottish politics, and the role that creative practices such as the remodeled Wallace monument and *Braveheart* will play in this future, will only become known as it is produced. Likewise, the connection between Welsh's fiction—Ross notes that Welsh now appears in the "expanded and more politically correct" (101) Hall of Heroes at the Wallace monument—and the future of Scotland remains to be determined.

Mark Renton, Roy Strang, and Bruce Robertson can be seen as three futures for Scotland. Of course, all three of these novel subjectivities are certainly "less savory" than one might hope for. But, with the "explosion" of "new Scottish writing," and the entry of Scotland into world politics, many more paths of moving from the known to the unknown are being produced by Welsh and other writers creating novel subjectivities. The new literature of Scotland has an indeterminate connection to the future of Scotland, but that does not mean that it is powerless or without force. Whatever the tenuous connections between the novel subjectivities produced by Welsh (and others associated with the "New Scottish writing") and the contemporary world of Scottish politics, both are actively, even deliriously, producing the future, whatever it may become.

# Conclusion: The Demand of Bartleby

*A belief that we know what teaching is or should be is actually a major impediment to just teaching.*

      —*Bill Readings,* The University in Ruins

In my introduction, I claim that an ethics of reading can have pedagogical force. At the same time, it seems difficult to say exactly how an ethics of reading works in the classroom. I can easily tell my students that an ethical reading is one in which a reader carefully considers how to respond to the otherness of a text, but, for most students, such a formulation is just going to be so many words. I can also lecture my students and minutely map out the work of fascinated disgust in Richard Powers or the importance of silence in Irvine Welsh. While such a lecturing may be of some use, it hardly seems to qualify as an ethical reading practice. Rather, for me, teaching an ethics of reading involves a seemingly paradoxical double movement: cultivating a space of fascination cut off from the wider world while at the same time arguing that literature, particularly contemporary literature, is relevant to everyday life.

Richard Powers offers a similar formulation of fiction's value. He says that "I happen to believe that the deepest value of fiction is that, in its very fictiveness, it is the one arena where we can, at least temporarily, take apart and refuse to compete within the terms that the rest of existence insists on" (Neilson 23). For Powers, fiction carves out a distinct space in the world, a space somehow removed from the demands of everyday life. The "value" of this space lies in what one can do there: examine, and "take apart" the workings of the world. Fiction, in a sense, provides a critical distance from the rest of the world. This formulation may seem to repeat some of the problems of the binary "inside/outside" understanding of literature that I discuss in my introduction. One crucial difference exists, though. Much literary criticism takes the inside/outside binary to be an inescapable structural feature of reading. Powers's formulation, and the double movement of an ethics of reading that I want to consider views the binary (whether inside/outside or fiction/world) as more of a temporal disjunction than a structural component. That is, Powers's claim that fiction allows us to "temporarily" cut off the world is key here. If fiction is to have any value, it cannot be a simple sanctuary from everyday life. Rather, fiction must always return to the world and must always bring something with it.

I view the classroom as a space that exists between fiction and the "rest of existence." It is in the space of the classroom, through the practice of reading, that fiction can be connected back to the world in some way. The classroom can function as a space where Powers's "refus[al] to compete" can be put into operation. In a classroom, students and teachers can slowly "take apart" a work and examine both the text and its context. In turn, this careful attention paid to text and context can then be used to further our understanding of how and why we create meanings, and the effects that these meanings produce. At the same time, there does not seem to be any basic model for moving from the space of literature to the wider world, for determining the limits of text and context, or for examining exactly how reading can engender a response to the otherness of a text.

In fact, the inability to construct a basic model or to make a general claim about how an ethics of reading works can be considered a key component of an ethics of reading. Just as I argue that an ethics of reading cannot precede an act of reading, I want to claim that an ethics of classroom practice cannot precede the acts of reading that take place in the classroom. Teaching an ethics of reading is a continual reinvention process. In his discussion of ethics and reading, J. Hillis Miller writes, "Exactly what in detail the establishment of a new ethics of reading might be like it would be presumptuous of me to try to spell out here" (*Ethics* 338). As I discuss in my introduction, for Miller, ethical readings always lead toward some kind of action, such as a teaching practice or critical work. These acts cannot be anticipated or figured beforehand; they are part of the process of reading, a component of Miller's "actual hard work of reading." To put it differently, and as I also discuss in my introduction, acts of reading produce what Deleuze calls "unforeseen and nonpreexistent" movements. These movements do not flow in one direction or toward a specific goal. Indeed, to dwell in literature's fascination is to dwell, at least temporarily, in a space of ignorance and fascination.

## Cultivating Fascination

Blanchot argues that reading has little to do with meaning, understanding, or comprehension. He writes that "reading, in the literary sense, is not even a pure movement of comprehension. It is not the interpretation that keeps meaning alive by pursuing it. Reading is situated beyond or before comprehension" (*Space* 196). Such a formulation of reading hardly seems the ground for any sort of pedagogical practice. Most students have been taught that reading is nothing but comprehension. Teaching an ethics of reading that follows Blanchot's formulation of reading involves a shift in focus from comprehension and understanding to ignorance and fascination. Blanchot writes,

> No one is gifted, be he author or reader, and whoever feels that he is feels primarily that he is not—feels infinitely ill equipped, absent from the power attributed to him. And just as to be an "artist" is not to know that art already exists, that this is already a world, so reading, seeing, hearing the work of art demands more ignorance than knowledge. It requires a knowledge endowed with an immense ignorance and a gift which is not given ahead of time, which has each time to be received and acquired in forgetfulness of it, and also lost. (*Space* 192)

Again, Blanchot's focus on "ignorance" and "forgetfulness" hardly seems the ground for any sort of classroom practice. How can one teach students to bring "an immense ignorance" to every act of reading? How can "forgetfulness" be taught to students who often want only to understand what a text means?

In *The University in Ruins,* Bill Readings points to the difficulties of teaching something other than pure comprehension. He argues that, as "the University is developing toward the status of a transnational corporation" (164), the question of the value of education is getting reconfigured. In this configuration, fiction's value as a space of slow, careful examination of the workings of the world gets displaced by a system in which "the question of the University is only the question of relative value-for-money, the question posed to a student who is situated entirely as a *consumer,* rather than as someone who wants to think" (27). The unforeseen and difficult-to-quantify value of reading gets superseded by a logic of production and consumption where value gets placed on that which is easily measurable through grading by professors and evaluation by students. Knowledge becomes important only as it can be fit into "the cycle of production, exchange, and consumption . . . so that the system can speculate on knowledge differentials, can profit from the accumulation of intellectual capital" (163–164). Within such a system, a pedagogy that aligns reading and thought with forgetfulness, ignorance, and fascination seems to have little immediate value.

There is a certain danger here of falling back into the kind of inside/outside dichotomy that I have been trying to escape throughout this book. I do not want to posit reading, in whatever form it takes, as the outside of a system of production and consumption. Nevertheless, if the guiding principle of reading were to become "value-for-money," even the "temporary" space of reading might be in jeopardy because it has no value that can be quantified. A logic of fascination is not necessarily a good business model. At the same time, it is not necessarily a good means of resistance to the increasing corporatization of the University. Reading, as an unforeseen response to a text, does not work toward an easily definable goal.

I cannot even say how to teach fascination, except to theorize that a good reading is not necessarily goal oriented, and that being unsure of exactly what is happening in a text is not necessarily bad. A teacher can encourage students to temporarily suspend the goals of meaning and understanding. Indeed, much contemporary fiction frustrates the kind of reading that would seek a complete understanding of a text. Readers never get a glimpse of any sort of inner life of Daitch's narrator in "Killer Whales," nor are they given enough information to clearly ascertain the story of her neighbor. In Powers's *Gain,* the two narrative threads never quite come together; the novel never says that the Clare corporation caused Laura Bodey's cancer. Welsh's *Trainspotting* and Wallace's *Infinite Jest* do not provide motivations for their characters' actions, nor do they resolve their stories. In teaching, I try to convince my students that these texts are not simply puzzles waiting for a good reader to solve them by discovering unity and understanding. At the same time, I strive to show students that postmodern narrative technique is not simply a reflection of a disjunctive, fragmentary world. Rather, I try to create a space where reading can dwell in fascination before making a return to everyday existence. Blanchot writes, "Reading is not a conversation; it does not discuss, it does not question. It never asks of the book, and still less of the author: 'What did you mean exactly? What truth, then, did you bring me?'" (*Space* 194). An ethical reading practice will not necessarily provide a student with a "truth" about the world, but it might encourage students to engage other ways of living, other logics that can be lived by.

If the ability to dwell in fascination can be taught, and I think it can, the second part of an ethical pedagogy seeks to return from this space of fascination with something "unforeseen and nonpreexistent," with a different way of considering the otherness encountered in fascination. In other words, an ethical reading practice must strive to make the goalless space of literature relevant to a wider world. An ethical reading should have something to say when it is no longer "temporarily" cut off from the rest of existence.

## Arguing Relevance

In *The Writing of the Disaster,* Blanchot critiques what he sees as the undue reverence often paid to works of art: "It is through reverence that the work, always already in ruins, is frozen: through reverence which prolongs, maintains, consecrates it (through the idolatry proper to titles), it congeals, or is added to the catalogue of the good works of culture" (80). Too much reverence can render a work into nothing more than a monument. Considering a work only within a rarefied realm of contemplation removes the work from a space of response. If a work of art is taken to inhabit an aesthetic space separated from the rest of the world, one cannot argue that the work has everyday relevance, let alone an ethical component. If works of art, and literature in this specific case, are to do anything, they must somehow inhabit the world of daily existence.

In my experience, students all too often think that literature has no value to the world outside the classroom. For this reason, I begin almost every literature class I teach (and especially "introduction to critical reading" classes) by putting the following quotation from Deleuze on the board: "The good ways of reading today succeed in treating a book like you would treat a record you listen to, a film or TV program you watch" (Deleuze and Parnet 3–4). Through a detailed interrogation of this claim, I encourage students to consider how we encounter various forms of media in everyday life, and how these encounters lead to the kinds of readings we produce. I ask my students how many of them have read a novel that was not assigned for a class in the last year. I then ask how many of them have watched a film or television show or listened to music in the past week. Of course, many more hands go up in response to the latter question. My point here is not to mourn the fact that "nobody reads anymore." Rather, I want to claim that, following Deleuze, a book can have just as much relevance as any other form of media. After speaking of the "good ways of reading," Deleuze continues by saying, "Any treatment of the book which claims for it a special respect—an attention of another kind—comes from another era and definitively condemns the book" (3–4). To a certain extent, such a claim is another way of saying, as many practitioners of cultural studies do, that literature is one discourse among others. At the same time, Deleuze's formulation does not just deprivilege the literary. To say that reading is "like" watching a film or listening to music also moves reading into the realm of everyday life. From such considerations, classroom practice can become not just a study of literature, but also a consideration of the ways that literature and contemporary culture intersect.

In discussing Deleuze's claim, I ask my students a series of questions: How do you treat a record? A TV show? A film? How do you treat a book? What are the different circumstances of each type of reading? Why do you read each of these things? What senses are involved in each occurrence? What is the physical experience in each case? What about the fact that we are reading this quote in an English class? Aren't we supposed to privilege books? Why might we want to deprivilege the literary text? Can we say anything about how these different modes of expression are usually considered? How they are consumed? What role might the marketplace play? The university setting? This line of questioning, I argue, is the beginning of a "good," critically engaged reading. Rather than setting out with the goal of saying what a text means, I encourage students to start with the context in which they are reading. Focusing on the specific scene of each act of reading can lead to a definition of reading as a series of negotiations among contexts. These negotiations can be considered ethical if readers pay close attention to the effects of their readings, to the ways of life that a response implies. Such a concept thinks of reading as an encounter with otherness that locates reading in an ethical register. Such an ethics need not be the exclusive terrain of either literary or cultural studies, and it can in fact negotiate among the two, and in turn bring an ethical force to the practice of teaching literature.

## The Demand of Bartleby

I do not want to end with a generalizable claim about the use of an ethics of reading. Rather, I want to return to, and expand on, a singular, seemingly incongruous, act of reading that I discuss in Chapter 1. Melville's "Bartleby the Scrivener" is the only noncontemporary work of literature that I have discussed. Part of the reason that I include "Bartleby" in my discussion of contemporary fiction can be attributed to intertextuality: Daitch's narrator makes a passing reference to "Bartleby," and Deleuze and Blanchot both write extensively about the story. More important than this intertextuality, though, I think of "Bartleby" as a difficult, if not perplexing, space of negotiation in the classroom.

The first time I taught this story, in a broad survey course called "The Short Story," discussion took an unexpected turn. A student voiced impatience with the story in general and with the narrator in particular. Why, this student wanted to know, doesn't the narrator simply fire Bartleby? He is an unproductive worker, and the narrator should feel no responsibility to him. That should be the end of the story. I could not say that this reading was incorrect or bad. Indeed, I found it hard to say exactly what responsibility the narrator did have for Bartleby. At the same time, the narrator undoubtedly has a deep fascination for Bartleby. My student, and this student was by no means alone in this regard, did not share the narrator's fascination. I could not disagree with this student's reading; the narrator's fascination with Bartleby is unaccountable. "Bartleby" is clearly not an effective business model.

In Chapter 1, I ask how readers might respond differently to Bartleby. Here, I want to reframe that question and ask, How can a teacher encourage students to respond differently to

Bartleby? It was easy enough to remind students that we were reading fiction and not a management manual. In a real-life situation, Bartleby would be out the door and probably forgotten. Temporarily suspending the judgments of a business-centered reading, I asked the class, What might we lose if we read "Bartleby" from only this perspective? More importantly, I asked, What can we get if we strive to read the story differently, if we place "Bartleby" back in the realm of fiction, and if we focus, temporarily, on the words on the page?

Shifted into a literary context, "Bartleby" becomes a difficult story to read. Close, careful attention to the text can show that, as the narrator says of Bartleby, "nothing is ascertainable" (Melville 3). Certainly, "Bartleby" can be, and has been, read as a rumination on Christian fellowship. The narrator notes that he cares about Bartleby, in part because "both I and Bartleby were sons of Adam" (17). He also notes that "to befriend Bartleby . . . will cost me little or nothing, while I lay up in my soul what will eventually prove a sweet morsel for my conscience" (13). At the same time, the narrator's feelings of fellowship for Bartleby are counterbalanced by a kid of repulsion, a desire to be rid of him. The narrator writes of "the suddenness and rapidity of my flight" (30) as he flees Bartleby; he also notes that "I had resolved to gather all my faculties together and forever rid me of this intolerable incubus" (27). More understatedly, he notes that "the passiveness of Bartleby sometimes irritated me" (13). This twin desire, to embrace Bartleby and to flee Bartleby, never gets resolved, largely because of Bartleby's massive indifference to any and all actions.

The story, in a sense, would prefer not to be read. It remains passive in the face of interpretation. Perhaps this passivity begins to explain why the story is so attractive to Deleuze, Blanchot, and Daitch. To read Bartleby is to read. That is, to formulate any response to Bartleby seems to involve a confrontation with the complete indifference of the text. The demand of reading compels readers to engage that indifference, to respond to it without neutralizing it. This line of reading, though, presents difficulties. Following this logic, a reader could end up in a de Manian dead end, where all that can be said is that "Bartleby" performs its own, and by allegorical extension, reading's, impossibility. Reading Bartleby as a cipher for all acts of reading can easily obscure the story's singularity.

In other words, to read "Bartleby" as a story of reading's impossibility covers over the inscrutable subjectivity of the "motionless young man" (Melville 8) who appears on the narrator's doorstep in answer to a call for a scrivener. Throughout the story, the narrator highlights just how difficult it is to know anything about Bartleby. He says that Bartleby is "the strangest [scrivener] I ever saw or heard of" (3); to the narrator, Bartleby "seemed alone, absolutely alone in the universe. A bit of wreck in the mid-Atlantic" (21). All of the narrator's attempts to explain Bartleby are blocked. Even the explanatory metaphoric power—"Dead letters! does it not sound like dead men?" (34)— of the narrator's final note that Bartleby was rumored to have worked at a dead letter office is undermined. The narrator reveals that he does not know where this rumor came from: "Upon what basis it rested, I could never ascertain" (33). Despite the narrator's best attempts, Bartleby remains unknown. In the classroom, I encourage students to remember the difficulties that this inscrutability brings to any interpretation of the story.

In a similar vein, Deleuze writes that "'Bartleby' is neither a metaphor for the writer nor the symbol of anything whatsoever" ("Bartleby" 68). "Bartleby" resists interpretation. To say that "Bartleby" is a story about business practice, or that it is an allegory of reading's impossibility, or that it is about Christian fellowship or the human condition is not "wrong." At the same time, to say that any of these interpretations offer a full understanding of the story covers over Bartleby's singularity. To offer any of these interpretations renders Bartleby into something familiar and sensible, something understandable. To say what "Bartleby" means necessitates forgetting that there is not "anything ordinarily human about him" (Melville 10).

Ultimately, I argue that an ethical reading of "Bartleby" does not reduce the story to an articulable meaning or understanding. My pedagogical goal is to convince students that reading can still work when it does not interpret. "Bartleby" is difficult, even impenetrable in a sense. It is impossible to reach a conclusion about, not because of any inherent ambiguity in the text that could somehow be resolved by an expert reader, but because the story remains indifferent to its readers, just as Bartleby asks nothing of the narrator at the end of the story. Bartleby, imprisoned in the Tombs, says to the narrator, "I know you . . . and I want nothing to say to you" (31). Likewise, the story itself wants to say "nothing" to its readers. It continually undermines interpretation with "pure, patient passivity." Meeting this passivity head on, without a goal of understanding it or transforming it into meaning, can be the beginning of an ethical reading practice. "Bartleby" continually blocks understanding. At the same time, this blockage can produce new lines of flight. In the classroom, I do not discourage acts of interpretation. Rather, I encourage students to produce readings that continually move in one direction and then die out. Not knowing where a reading is going is not a reason to cut off that reading. In fact, reading without a goal of saying what a text means is a key component of an ethics of reading. In teaching "Bartleby," I strive to create the conditions of emergence for the singular, inhuman, and passive subjectivity of the title character. I encourage students to attempt to produce lines of flight in and through the story and to decide what responsibilities these lines entail. I encourage students to carefully analyze how and why they respond to "Bartleby," and to consider the effects of their responses. These responses are often boredom and frustration brought on by "Bartleby's" passivity. "Bartleby's" passive indifference to readers is not the end of reading. It is the beginning.

# Notes

## Introduction

1. Mailloux writes, "There are various ways to trouble the neat narrative I have just told about reader-response criticism" (77).
2. I will not rehearse here the differences between de Man's use of deconstuction and Derrida's. See Nealon's discussion, "The Commodification of Deconstruction in America" (27–41), in *Double Reading*.
3. His reading of Proust can be taken as exemplary for all reading, as de Man states: "But there is absolutely no reason why analyses of the kind here suggested for Proust would not be applicable, with proper modifications of techniques, to Milton, or to Dante or to Holderin" (16–17).
4. See "Literary Theory at the Present Time," where Miller writes that "there is a fully elaborated theory of the historical, psychological and ethical relation of literature already present, for example, in de Man's *Allegories of Reading*" (387).
5. As I write this, though, more and more critics are forging connections between Deleuze and postmodern literature. See, for instance, John Marks' and Claire Colebrook's essays on, respectively, Don DeLillo and Bret Easton Ellis in *Deleuze and Literature*.
6. Upon the reprint of "The Cultural Logic of Late Capitalism" (from 1984) in *Postmodernism*, Jameson notes that, in 1990, the essay has "the additional interest as an historical document" (xvi).
7. See also Linda Hutcheon's review of three books of postmodern literary criticism in *Contemporary Literature*, in which she uses language similar to McHale's: "Like every other book on this topic, [these authors] have to deal with Jameson's early theorizing of the 'cultural logic of late capitalism'" (170). Also, Katherine Hayles considers "Jameson's theory of postmodernism [to be] perhaps the single most influential work on the subject to date" (*How We* 286); and Paul Maltby notes that "Jameson's *Postmodernism* [is] arguably the *locus classicus* of the postmodernism debate" (8).
8. See also Maltby: "Jameson's inability to ascribe critical effectivity to postmodernist art must be understood, ultimately, in the context of his model of late capitalist society as a fundamentally stable formation" (12).

9. Geoffrey Lord's discussion sums up this point of view; he writes that many critics "have advanced the view that postmodernism should not be thought of as a monolithic concept, and that it is better to speak of 'postmodernisms'" (10). Likewise, Simmons argues for a fluid definition of postmodernism under the rubric "some definitions": "But what *can* meaningfully be called postmodern? One approaches a term as large and ungainly as 'postmodernism' the way the blind men approached the elephant. Each took hold of a different part and described a different beast" (5).

# Chapter 1

1. A bracket that I'll later open in discussion of David Markson.
2. Ignoring, for now, everything that happens in between these two moments.
3. Derrida asks, rhetorically, "What would a mark be that could not be cited?" ("Signature" 12).
4. She briefly returns to this reference later.
5. It is telling of the novel's plotlessness that Kate tells the reader nothing of how this situation came about; *Wittgenstein's Mistress* is no *The Omega Man* or *The Day After*.
6. Not knowing that baseball was often played on artificial surfaces starting in the 1970s, she types lengthy digressions on just what that title could mean.
7. In "Reviewers in Flat Heels: Being a Postface to Several Novels," Markson takes his reviewers to task for not being as erudite as he is. After mentioning some canonical modernist texts that he often refers to, Markson asks, "Can most reviewers of this stripe actually read those benchmark texts with comfort, even today?" (128).
8. She mentions *Wuthering Heights* only two other times. She says, "At first glance one would scarcely have expected *Wuthering Heights* to be a book about windows, either" (63); She also says, "Emily Bronte never once had a lover. / Which is presumably an explanation for why so many people in *Wuthering Heights* are continually looking in and out of windows, in fact. / Or climbing in and out of them, even" (97).
9. Kate often speaks of windows; see, for example, 42, 46–47, 56, 62–63, 134, and many more places.

# Chapter 2

1. See, for example, Paul de Man's reading of Blanchot, "Impersonality in the Criticism of Maurice Blanchot," in *Blindness and Insight*, 60–78.

2. The wide range of responses to *Gain* can serve as an example of criticism moving too quickly toward a judgment. Powers speaks of the critical reception of *Gain*: "The diversity of responses to that book amazes me. The readings ranged not only across a gamut of likes and dislikes, but across an interpretive spectrum of entirely incommensurable readings, as if they were referring to completely different books. One reviewer called the book a one-note bashing of corporate existence. Another claimed that the book was a glorification of contemporary corporate capital-ism. One writer said that the book lacked a vision of evil, but another said that I came down too hard and unsubtly on the insidious corporate evil. Several reviews commented on my new depth of characterization, but others spoke of a cold indiffer-ence to character" (J. Williams 10).

3. A goalless voyage only to a certain degree: "So long as research's goal fell in sea-lanes so full of shrimp and fish, com-merce was a great believer in research" (53).

4. As they tell him "we only sent you to university in the first place in the mistaken belief that the cost of your edification would someday cease to be a drain and begin to return something to the family's current account" (71).

5. I put "Richard Powers" in quotation marks to differentiate between the novel's narrator and author.

6. Her first quitting was brought on by a news story about a racial hate crime, in which a motorist beat another driver into a coma with a tire iron. After reading this story, Helen says to "Powers," "I don't want to play anymore" (314). Yet she does make a brief return, to write her answer to the exam.

# Chapter 3

1. From the synopsis in footnote 24: "The figure of Death . . . presides over the front entrance of a carnival sideshow whose spectators watch performers undergo unspeakable degradations so grotesquely compelling that the spectators' eyes become larger and larger until the spectators themselves are transformed into gigantic eyeballs in chairs, while on the other side of the sideshow tent the figure of Life . . . uses a megaphone to invite fairgoers to an exhibition in which, if the fairgoers consent to undergo unspeakable degradations, they can witness ordinary persons gradually turn into gigantic eyeballs" (988).

2. Deleuze and Guattari cite the following line from "A Report to the Academy": "'There was no attraction for me in imitating

    human beings; I imitated them because I needed a way out, and for no other reason'" (*Kafka* 14).

3. We never learn the first name of Steeply's father.

4. It should be noted that Steeply's mother's use of prescription antianxiety medication helps make this situation possible.

5. A footnote transcribing scores of indecipherable notebooks written in "a kind of medical-slash-military-looking code" (646) might try the patience even of a champion of "radical realism."

6. Making this connection stronger, the wraith also puts "ghost-words" into Gately's head—that is, words that Gately has never heard before suddenly appear in his mind. Most of these words are either physics- or cinema-related—"NEUTRAL DENSITY POINT, CHIAROSCURO . . . and ANNULATE and BRICO-LAGE . . . and SCOPOPHILIA" (832, capitals in the original)—but the wraith also forces "LAERTES" and "POOR YORICK" (832) into Gately's head.

# Chapter 4

1. And this emergence takes place "within shared existence." Blanchot does not, as Schwartz writes, "effect a radical separation of art and world" (Schwartz 21). Indeed, the writer is one who precisely keeps these two worlds in touch, as Blanchot writes, "through language, in language." "To write is to let fascination rule language. It is to stay in touch, through language, in language, with the absolute milieu where the thing becomes image again, where the image . . . becomes an allusion to the featureless, and instead of a form drawn upon absence, becomes the formless presence of this absence, the opaque, empty opening onto that which is when there is no more world, when there is no world yet"(*Space* 33).

2. See *Children of Albion Rovers, Acid Plaid,* and *The Vintage Book of Contemporary Scottish Fiction.*

# WORKS CITED

Annesley, James. *Blank Fictions: Consumerism, Culture and the Contemporary American Novel*. New York: St. Martin's Press, 1998.

Blanchot, Maurice. "Kafka and Literature." *The Work of Fire*. Trans. Charlotte Mandell. Stanford: Stanford UP, 1995. 12–26.

———. "Literature and the Right to Death." *The Work of Fire*. 300–344.

———. *The Space of Literature*. Trans. Ann Smock. Lincoln: U of Nebraska P, 1982.

———. *The Writing of The Disaster*. Trans. Ann Smock. Lincoln: U of Nebraska P, 1995.

Brenkman, John. "Extreme Criticism." *What's Left of Theory: New Work on the Politics of Literary Theory*. Ed. Judith Butler, John Guillory, and Kendall Thomas. New York: Routledge, 2000. 114–136.

Calder, Angus. "By the Water of Leith I Sat Down and Wept: Reflections on Scottish Identity." *Acid Plaid: New Scottish Writing*. Ed. Harry Ritchie. New York: Arcade Publishing, 1997. 218–238.

Daitch, Susan. "Killer Whales." *Storytown*. Normal, IL: Dalkey Archive P, 1996. 9–17.

Davis, Lennard J. "Forum." *PMLA* 112.2 (March 1997): 257–286.

Deleuze, Gilles. "Bartleby; or the Formula." *Essays Critical and Clinical*. Trans. Daniel W. Smith and Michael A. Greco. Minneapolis: U of Minnesota P, 1997. 68–90.

———. "Gilles Deleuze and Felix Guattari on *A Thousand Plateaus*." *Negotiations*. 25–34.

———. "Life as a Work of Art." *Negotiations*. 94–101.

———. "Literature and Life." *Essays Critical and Clinical*. 1–6.

———. "Letter to A Harsh Critic." *Negotiations*. 3–12.

———. *Nietzsche and Philosophy*. Trans. Hugh Tomlinson. New York: Columbia UP, 1993.

———. "On Philosophy." *Negotiations*. 135–155.

———. "A Portrait of Foucault." *Negotiations*. 102–118.

———. "Preface to the French Edition." *Essays Critical and Clinical*. lv–lvi.

Deleuze, Gilles, and Felix Guattari. *Kafka, Toward a Minor Literature*. Trans. Dana Polan. Minneapolis: U of Minnesota P, 1986.

———. *A Thousand Plateaus: Capitalism and Schizophrenia*. Trans. Brian Massumi. Minneapolis: U of Minnesota P, 1987.

———. *What Is Philosophy?* Trans. Hugh Tomlinson and Graham Burchell. New York: Columbia UP, 1994.

Deleuze, Gilles, and Claire Parnet. *Dialogues*. Trans. Hugh Tomlinson and Barbara Habberjam. New York: Columbia UP, 1987.

DeLillo, Don. *Underworld*. New York: Scribner, 1997.

De Man, Paul. *Allegories of Reading: Figural Language in Rousseau, Nietzsche, Rilke, and Proust*. New Haven: Yale UP, 1979.

———. *Blindness and Insight: Essays in the Rhetoric of Contemporary Criticism*. Minneapolis: U of Minnesota P, 1983.

Derrida, Jacques. "Limited Inc a b c." *Limited Inc*. Ed. Gerald Graff. Trans. Samuel Weber. Evanston, IL: Northwestern UP, 1988. 29–111.

———."Signature Event Context." *Limited Inc*. 1–24.

Doyle, Richard. *Wetwares: Experiments in Postvital Living*. Minneapolis: U of Minnesota P, 2003.

Edwards, Brian. *Theories of Play in Postmodern Theory*. New York: Garland Publishing, 1998.

Fish, Stanley. *Is There a Text in This Class? The Authority of Interpretive Communities*. Cambridge, MA: Harvard UP, 1980.

Foucault, Michel. "Nietzsche, Genealogy, History." *Language, Counter-memory, Practice: Selected Essays and Interviews*. Ed. Donald F. Bouchard. Trans. Donald F. Bouchard and Sherry Simon. Ithaca: Cornell UP, 1977. 139–164.

Freeman, Alan. "Ghosts in Sunny Leith: Irvine Welsh's *Trainspotting*." *Studies in Scottish Fiction: 1945 to the Present*. Ed. Susan Hageman. New York: Peter Lang, 1997. 251–262.

Frith, Simon. "On Not Being Scottish." *Critical Quarterly*. 42.4 (2000): 1–6.

Grace, Sherrill E. "Messages: Reading *Wittgenstein's Mistress*." *Review of Contemporary Fiction*. 10.2 (1990): 207–216.

Guattari, Félix. *Chaosmosis: An Ethico-Aesthetic Paradigm*. Trans. Paul Bains and Julian Pefanis. Bloomington: Indiana UP, 1995.

Hageman, Susan, ed. "Introduction." *Studies in Scottish Fiction: 1945 to the Present*. 7–15.

Hardt, Michael, and Antonio Negri. *Empire*. Cambridge, MA: Harvard UP, 2000.

Harris, Charles B. "'The Stereo View': Politics and the Role of the Reader in *Gain*." *Review of Contemporary Fiction* 18.3 (Fall 1998): 97–108.

Hayles, N. Katherine. *Chaos Bound: Orderly Disorder in Contemporary Literature and Science*. Ithaca: Cornell UP, 1990.

———. *How We Became Posthuman: Virtual Bodies in Cybernetics, Literature and Informatics*. Chicago: U of Chicago P, 1999.

———. "The Illusion of Autonomy and the Fact of Recursivity: Virtual Ecologies, Entertainment and *Infinite Jest*." *New Literary History* 30.3 (1999): 675–697.

Howard, Gerald. "A *Trainspotting* Glossary." *Paris Review* 38 (Spring 1996): 348–349.

Hutcheon, Linda. "Once Again, from the Top: More Pomo Promo." *Contemporary Literature* 36.1 (Spring 1995): 164–172.

Jameson, Fredric. *Postmodernism, or the Cultural Logic of Late Capitalism*. Durham: Duke UP, 1991.

Kafka, Franz. "The Metamorphosis." *The Complete Stories*. Trans. Willa and Edwin Muir. New York: Shocken, 1971. 89–139.

Kravitz, Peter. "Introduction." *The Vintage Book of Contemporary Scottish Fiction*. Ed. Peter Kravitz. New York: Vintage Books, 1999. xi–xxxvi.

Lambert, Gregg. "On the Uses and Abuses of Literature for Life." *Deleuze and Literature*. Ed. Ian Buchanan and John Marks. Edinburgh: Edinburgh UP, 2000. 135–166.

LeClair, Tom. "The Prodigious Fiction of Richard Powers, William Vollman, and David Foster Wallace." *Critique* 38.1 (Fall 1996): 12–37.

Lord, Geoffrey. *Postmodernism and Notions of National Difference: A Comparison of Postmodern Fiction in Britain and America*. Atlanta: Rodopi P, 1996.

Mailloux, Steven. *Reception Histories: Rhetoric, Pragmatism, and American Cultural Politics*. Ithaca: Cornell UP, 1998.

Maltby, Paul. *Dissident Postmodernists: Barthelme, Coover, Pynchon*. Philadelphia: U of Pennsylvania P, 1991.

Markson, David. *Reader's Block*. Normal, IL: Dalkey Archive P, 1996.

———. "Reviewers in Flat Heels: Being a Postface to Several Novels." *Review of Contemporary Fiction* 10.2 (1990): 124–130.

———. *Wittgenstein's Mistress*. Normal, IL: Dalkey Archive P, 1995.

McHale, Brian. *Constructing Postmodernism*. New York: Routledge, 1992.

———. "Postmodernism, Or the Anxiety of Master Narratives." *Diacritics* 22.1 (Spring 1992): 17–33.

———. *Postmodernist Fiction*. New York: Routledge, 1987.

Melville, Herman. "Bartleby the Scrivener." New York: Dover Thrift Editions, 1990.

Miklitsch, Robert. "Forum." *PMLA* 112.2 (March 1997): 257–286.

Miller, J. Hillis. *The Ethics of Reading: Kant, Eliot, Trollope, James, and Benjamin*. New York: Columbia UP, 1987.

———. "The Function of Literary Theory at the Present Time." *The Future of Literary Theory*. Ed. Ralph Cohen. New York: Routledge, 1989. 102–111.

Mitchell, Chris. "The Agony and the Ecstasy." *Spike Magazine*. 1997. http://www.spikemagazine.com/1000agonyandecstasy.php (accessed October 18, 2000).

Moore, Steven. "Afterword." *Wittgenstein's Mistress*. Normal, IL: Dalkey Archive P, 1995. 243–248.

Morrow, Bradford, and Richard Powers. "A Dialogue: Richard Powers and Bradford Morrow." *Conjunctions* 34.4 (Spring 2000): 1–9.

Murphy, Timothy S. *Wising Up the Marks: The Amodern William Burroughs*. Los Angeles: U of California P, 1997.

Nealon, Jeffrey, T. *Double Reading: Postmodernism after Deconstruction*. Ithaca: Cornell UP, 1993.

Neilson, Jim. "An Interview with Richard Powers." *Review of Contemporary Fiction* 18.3 (Fall 1998): 13–23.

Nelson, Cary. "Forum." *PMLA* 112.2 (1997): 257–286.

Newton, Adam Zachary. *Narrative Ethics*. Cambridge, MA: Harvard UP, 1995.

Pezzolano, Hebert Benítez. "Resistance to Literature." *Substance* 92 (2000): 94–99.

Powers, Richard. Gain. New York: Farrar, Straus, and Giroux, 1998.

———. *Galatea 2.2*. New York: HarperCollins, 1995.

———. *The Gold Bug Variations*. New York: HarperCollins, 1991.

———. *Operation Wandering Soul*. New York: HarperCollins, 1993.

———. *Plowing the Dark*. New York: Farrar, Straus, and Giroux, 2000.

———. *Prisoner's Dilemma*. New York: HarperCollins, 1988.

———. *Three Farmers on Their Way to a Dance*. New York: HarperCollins, 1985.

Readings, Bill. *The University in Ruins*. Cambridge, MA: Harvard UP, 1995.

Ritchie, Harry, ed. "Introduction." *Acid Plaid*. 1–4.

Ross, Andrew. "Wallace's Monument and the Resumption of Scotland." *Social Text* 18.4 (Winter 2000): 83–107.

Schwartz, Stephen Adam. "Faux Pas: Maurice Blanchot on the Ontology of Literature." *Substance* 85 (1998): 19–47.

Shankar, S. "Forum." *PMLA* 112.2 (1997): 257–286.

Shaviro, Steven. *The Cinematic Body*. Minneapolis: U of Minnesota P, 1993.

Simmons, Philip E. *Deep Surfaces: Mass Culture and History in Postmodern American Fiction*. Athens: U of Georgia P, 1997.

Strecker, Trey. "Ecologies of Knowledge: The Encyclopedic Narratives of Richard Powers and His Contemporaries." *Review of Contemporary Fiction* 18.3 (Fall 1998): 67–71.

Sullivan, Evelin E. "*Wittgenstein's Mistress* and the Art of Connections." *Review of Contemporary Fiction* 10.2 (1990): 240–246.

Tabbi, Joseph. "Fiction to the Second Powers." *Node 9: An E-Journal of Writing and Technology*. July 4, 2000. http://vallejo.phil3.uni-freiburg.de/2000/tabbi.html.

———. David Markson: An Introduction." *Review of Contemporary Fiction* 10.2 (1990): 91–102.

———. "An Interview with David Markson." *Review of Contemporary Fiction* 10.2 (1990): 104–117.

———. *Postmodern Sublime: Technology and American Writing from Mailer to Cyberpunk*. Ithaca: Cornell UP, 1995.

———."Solitary Inventions: David Markson at the End of the Line." *Modern Fiction Studies* 43.3 (Fall 1997): 745–772.

Tompkins, Jane, ed. *Reader-Response Criticism: From Formalism to Post-structuralism*. Baltimore: Johns Hopkins UP, 1980.

Wallace, David Foster. *Brief Interviews with Hideous Men*. New York: Little, Brown, 1999.

———. "The Empty Plenum: David Markson's *Wittgenstein's Mistress*." *Review of Contemporary Fiction* 10.2 (1990): 217–239.

———. *Infinite Jest*. New York: Little, Brown, 1996.

Walsh, Richard. *Novel Arguments: Reading Innovative American Fiction*. New York: U of Cambridge P, 1995.

Welsh, Irvine. *The Acid House*. New York: Norton, 1994.

———. *Filth*. New York: Norton, 1998

———. *Marabou Stork Nightmares*. New York: Norton, 1996.

———. "The Rosewell Incident." *Children of Albion Rovers: New Scottish Writing*. Ed. Kevin Williamson. Woodstock, NY: Overlook P, 1997. 171–228.

———. *Trainspotting*. London: Minerva, 1993.

Williams, Jeffrey. "The Last Generalist: An Interview with Richard Powers." *Cultural Logic* 2.2 (Spring 1999). http://www.eserver.org/clogic/2-2/williams.html.

Williams, Raymond. *Marxism and Literature*. Oxford: Oxford UP, 1997.

Williamson, Kevin. "Team Talk." *Children of Albion Rovers: New Scottish Writing*. 1–3.